WINNING

IN THE BATTLES OF LIFE

WORKBOOK

Discover Keys to Victory

By Joan E. Murray

This workbook is designed to provide accurate and authoritative information with regard to the subject matter covered. This information is given with the understanding that neither the author nor Joan Murray Ministries is engaged in rendering legal, professional advice. Since the details of your situation are fact dependent, you should additionally seek the services of a competent professional.

Printed in the United States of America

Other Books by Author

Flow Through Me, Lord

Called and Chosen for Destiny

Workbook: Called and Chosen for Destiny

Show Me How to Love

Faith that Conquers

Hope in Difficult Seasons

I Must Pray

Lord, Make Me Whole

Lord, Make Me Whole (Spanish)

Overcoming Loneliness and Aloneness

Reconnect

Boldness in Christ

Time In Life's Waiting Room

Winning In the Battles of Life

Workbook: Winning in the Battles of Life

Worship Our Deepest Need

You Can Trust Him

Workbook: You Can Trust Him

Other Resources

https://joanmurrayministries.org/
https://jemmuniquegifts.com
https://linktr.ee/joanmurrayministries

My gift to you
PRAYERS That Produce Results
https://joanmurrayministries.org/prayers/praying-the-word-of-god/

Table of Contents

INTRODUCTION

You win!

As I think about the word winning, I must reflect on the many times I have found myself in difficult life situations where it appeared that winning was not an option. My difficulties seemed insurmountable, and I felt as if I was in an uphill struggle with no one to help me get to the top. As I struggled and fought, there was always a still small voice, whispering, "You can make it!" During those times the Lord would remind me that the battles have already been won on my behalf, and all I had to do was go in and gather all the spoils of war that Jesus won for me. The battles have also been won on your behalf, and the goods are waiting for you to come in and gather them.

Some of you have endured severe hardship. You have been embroiled in many life battles and cannot see a way out, but it is possible for you to win because Jesus made you a winner. The enemy has attacked your mind, body, emotions, and relationships. It seems as if he is winning, but it is impossible for him to win because the winning power of the Holy Spirit lives in you. The attacks of the enemy are designed to get your eyes off your Source, Jesus, and get you to focus on the enemy thus missing the help Jesus provides. When you are overcome with worry, dread, and fear, you are giving your power away to the enemy because your focus is on him. However, when you praise, worship, give thanks, and simply trust in God, you focus on Him; and, as He receives the worship, you will experience the breakthroughs in your life.

As Christians, we are on the battlefield. Since the battles are raging, you must be equipped for them. God has given each believer battle gear to protect and to fortify us in battle. He has provided a helmet of salvation; a breastplate of righteousness; and a belt of truth. He has dressed your feet with the gospel of peace; given you a shield of faith; a sword of the Spirit, which is the Word of God; and He tells you He is warring for you, and you will win. A key component to winning the battles is to develop spiritual muscles that will give you the endurance to outlast the devil. The devil knows he cannot conquer you and ultimately succeed because Jesus defeated and dethroned him his only hope is to outlast you in the battles you face. You must decide you have more determination and tenacity than he does; and no matter the length of the battle or the struggles you face, you will be the victor. You will not only outlast the devil, but you must also be determined, disciplined, consistent, and have the tenacity to win and to win every time. This book is filled with keys for overcoming and winning each battle you face. As you read, meditate, prepare, and apply these principles, you will find yourself in the winners' circle receiving the reward for all you have endured. Run to win!

Do you not know that in a race all the runners run, but only one gets the prize? Run in such a way as to get the prize. Everyone who competes in the games goes into strict training. They do it to get a crown that will not last; but we do it to get a crown that will last forever. 1 Corinthians 9:24 – 25 (NIV)

Joan E. Murray
Founder, Joan Murray Ministries

You win!

Winning
Chapter 1

The key to being victorious in every situation you encounter is to know that God has made you a winner in life. It is impossible to tell you how to win the battles of life without first telling you that you have already won – declare it "I am a winner!" You win in every situation you face and in every battle you encounter! You win because Jesus, through His obedience to God the Father, has already won the victory for you because of His unselfish act of dying on the cross of Calvary. In the book of Second Kings is a story of how God fights and wins the battles on your behalf. Second Kings chapter seven tells the story of four lepers who lived in Samaria, a city that was experiencing famine because the king of Aram had besieged it. They decided to leave the city and go into the Arameans' camp and surrender themselves in the hope of receiving help and finding food to survive the famine. When they arrived, the camp was empty because the Lord God had caused the Arameans to hear what sounded like a great army and their chariots and horses, so they fled their tents in fear. They abandoned all they had – food, gold, silver, and clothing - and ran for their lives. When the lepers arrived, they found an abundance of everything they needed and more. God had provided abundantly for them. The lepers decided that it was not right to keep the good news of the bounty to themselves, so they went back and reported to the people that the Arameans had fled, and God had provided abundantly for them. The people of God went into the Arameans' camp and gathered the goods God had so graciously provided by His power and might.

The scriptures make it clear God has already supplied all your needs even in the midst of the battle. You must learn to stand still, allow the Lord to fight your battles for you, and then go in and gather the blessings He provides. Many of you have encountered some devastating and traumatic times. The enemy has shot poison arrows which caused severe damage to your mind and your plans. The surprising thing is, when encountering these deadly events, most people are unaware they are engaged in a battle. They do not know how to fight or position themselves to overcome and gain the victory. Know that God always wants you to win and triumph in all areas of your life.

God has filled you with His presence and embraced you with His love and power while making the deposit of a conqueror in your heart. He has given you a Counselor, an Advocate, and a Helper in the person of the Holy Spirit to ensure your success; and, as you seek His help, you will become more than a conqueror through Christ Jesus who loves you (Romans 8:37). You can face every battle knowing you have already won, and you are an overcomer. You overcome by the blood of the Lamb and the word of your testimony (Revelation 12:11). Your testimony is you can do all things through Christ who strengthens you. You will obtain your testimony because of the battles you fight and win. Someone once said without a 'test' there is no testimony. You will be tested but you will prevail.

_____

_____

_____

_____

_____

_____

_____

_____

_____

Run To Win

Do you not know that in a race all the runners run, but only one gets the prize? Run in such a way as to get the prize. Everyone who competes in the games goes into strict training. They do it to get a crown that will not last; but we do it to get a crown that will last forever. Therefore I do not run like a man running aimlessly; I do not fight like a man beating the air. No, I beat my body and make it my slave so that after I have preached to others, I myself will not be disqualified for the prize. 1 Corinthians 9:24 – 27 (NIV)

These questions are worth asking. What race are you running? What do you hope to gain? What are you willing to do to gain the prize? The Apostle Paul gives a clear picture of the cost of winning a race in life. Each one of you has a race you must run. You determine if you will win or lose. To win and gain the prize, you must discipline your mind and your body. You must train your mind with the Word of God so you will not be disqualified by the attacks the enemy brings against you. Train yourself to endure and persevere when you encounter daily trials and tribulations. Know without a doubt there is a reason for your life and run the race not aimlessly but with a destination and purpose in mind.

The word 'race' in Greek means "stadion" from which we get our English word stadium. The Apostle Paul compares our race with an Olympian. The winner of an Olympic race is rewarded financially and with great honor. How often have you watched the Olympic games and observed the winner standing on the podium while their national anthem is being played? It is important to note in order for them to be in the winners' circle, they had to be people of determination, extremely disciplined in their lifestyle, balanced in their outlook, and totally committed to excellence. They had one destination in mind and that was to be the first one at the finish line and to be in the winners' circle. Once they made it to the finish line, they knew the prize was theirs. They would be crowned the winner. They also knew all eyes would be focused on them because they had gone the distance, endured the trials, overcome the pain, disappointments, and often the discouragement which came when they determined to succeed and make a difference in their life and the lives of others.

After enduring, they finally made it to their goal and attained the great prize they were pursuing. This analogy applies to you as well. You must endure, you must overcome, you must push disappointments aside, and race to the finish line knowing that there is a great prize waiting for you in the winners' circle. You will receive the blessings, the promises, and the rewards God gives to those who endure to the end because He is with you in this race of life. God will always make sure that the outcome of the race is in your favor.

What am I doing to gain the prize?

_____

_____

_____

_____

_____

_____

Prayer For Determination

Father, in the name of Jesus I thank You for every person who will decide today to get in the game of life. I ask You to make it crystal clear to their hearts the battles have been won and the victory is theirs. Let no weapon that is formed against them ever prosper. They overcome by the blood of the Lamb and the word of their testimony. They can do all things through Christ who strengthens them. They are victorious in all things because the Victor lives in them. I speak to their hearts and call forth courage, boldness, tenacity, assurance, and peace in the name of Jesus. I ask You to crown all their efforts with success. Shelter them under Your protection. Teach them what to do in every battle they face. Cause them to be blessed beyond measure as they determine not to give up, cave in, or give way to the devil. Show them because You are for them, nothing can succeed against them, and they will win every time. Let them understand the Greater One lives in them, and they have the power and the backing of the Holy Spirit governing their lives. This person who is the Holy Spirit, is their comforter, protector, guide, and advocate (lawyer). In Jesus' name I thank You that You will give them understanding of the tools and keys to winning and to success. We declare this to be so in Jesus' name. *Amen!* (So be it).

Keys for Winning
Chapter 2

Determination

Therefore, my beloved brethren, be ye steadfast, immovable, always abounding in the work of the Lord, forasmuch as ye know that your labor is not in vain in the Lord. Corinthians 15:58 (KJV)

To attain the victory and get the right outcome in battles, you must decide and then resolve in your heart you will win. Determination makes you steadfast and immovable. It gives you the courage to stand boldly and take the steps that will lead you to your desired destination. You must conclude in your mind you will not settle for less than what God has for you. Consider the many times you were faced with tough choices and wanted to give up. You could not see the light at the end of the tunnel, but you pressed on anyway. You knew life had more to offer, and you decided to stick with it. You won the round because you refused to give up or give in. Determined people will always win because losing is not an option for them.

In the above scripture, the Apostle Paul encourages us to be steadfast, immovable, firm, constant, and unwavering in our determination to win. This is the attitude you need to succeed. In the life of every achiever, you will find they share something in common. They are determined to succeed and are unshakeable in their belief and in their faith that they will. The outcome they seek is not negotiable to them. They know what they are pursuing and are determined to gain the reward. The word steadfast means to be stationary – it is remaining in one place for an extended period. It also means you are firm and steady. Often when you think of steadfastness, you think of a foundation that is strong, secure, and durable. This is our foundation in Christ. It is strong, secure, and durable (long lasting).

The Apostle Paul is asking you to be unshakeable in your belief and in your faith, and to be dependable and reliable in your commitment. God invites you to build a solid Christ centered foundation and to be a rock of refuge to others, so you can demonstrate to them how to hold fast to what they believe. When a person is dependable and reliable, others know they can be trusted to follow through, and to be an anchor for them in the battles of life. Paul also gives us a clear picture of what it means to be immovable. The word immovable suggests people who are unbending in their character unchangeable in their nature; and those who are not easily moved from their stance or from the position they have taken. To win and become the achiever God created you to be, as you face the battles of life, you must become fixed on the goal. You must be grounded in your belief about who God is in your life and what He accomplished for you through the death of His Son;

and the outcome for you will be success. Your success will come because you have anchored your soul, your life, and your plans in the immovable rock of Jesus Christ. You must be convinced in His presence and as part of His family, you are firmly established and reside permanently in Him. With this attitude of a victor, you will win and become more than a conqueror each time.

What does determination mean to me and how determined am I to win?

_____

_____

_____

_____

_____

_____

_____

_____

Discipline

He openeth also their ear to discipline, and commandeth that they return from iniquity. If they obey and serve Him, they shall spend their days in prosperity, and their years in pleasures. Job 36:1011 (KJV)

I can almost hear the sighs and the groans emanating from most of you as you read the word 'discipline'. You are already envisioning the work ahead of you, as you take hold of this needed key for winning. It is important to note the word 'discipline' comes from the word disciple. The term disciple is used often in the New Testament by Jesus to describe His followers. Since that is the case, let's explore what this means to you as you prepare yourself to become one of His disciples.

A disciple is a scholar and a learner. It depicts a person who believes in the doctrine of his teacher and follows the doctrine closely. All of you are disciples of Jesus Christ because you follow Him daily and learn from Him. He is the One you model your life after. Jesus was a disciple of God the Father. He modeled His example for us. He spoke only what the Father told Him to say and did only what He was instructed to do. He depended on His Father and was totally interconnected to God. The same applies to the Holy Spirit. He models the life of Jesus for us. He does what Jesus instructs Him to do and He leads you based on the instructions He receives from the Father and the Son. To be disciplined in your walk with Christ, you must become one of His disciples. To be victorious in the battles you face, you must be willing to go through the process of being 'remade' into the image of Christ. This remaking means to be conformed into the image of God's Son (Romans 8:29). To be 'remade', you will often experience some stretching to develop strong muscles, which will enable you to endure the race.

As these muscles are being developed, there is often some tightness, soreness and even some pain associated with it. The reason for this is that many of the muscles have not been exercised they have been lying dormant, so when pressure is applied to them you feel the strain. The problem occurs the moment you feel any discomfort and think you are not in God's will. Others think this could not be His plan for you, so you do not proceed any further with the exercise. Jesus said that anyone who comes after Him must deny himself, take up his cross daily, and follow Him (Matthew 16:24). This indicates that there may be some pressure, pain, and discomfort required of you to grasp all that you desire from Him. Jesus used the term "Take up your cross," because it gives a clear indication of what you may have to endure, as you make the decision to deny yourself in your desire to follow Him. When you and I let go of self, we are then able to embrace Him, and become more and more like Him in every way. Without His commitment to God and His discipline to adhere to everything God gave Him to accomplish by way of the cross, we would be lost and without hope. Discipline kept Jesus moving forward even though He was fully aware of the sufferings He would endure not only on the way to the cross but also during the crucifixion.

Let me define the word discipline. It means to be trained, to practice, to be restrained, to exert control, and to receive correction. Have you ever met a person who is extremely disciplined? If you have, and have come to know them well, you will usually find that they are disciplined in many areas of their life not just in one specific area. When you train to be disciplined in an area, that practice of discipline will overflow into all the other areas of your life. This is because the practice of discipline teaches you to be restrained and to exert control in whatever you decide to do. It takes a person of discipline to run the race of life and to win. Discipline will keep you in the race long after others have thrown in the towel and given up. Discipline develops stamina to keep you going even though the going might be tougher than you bargained for.

In what areas of my life am I disciplined? How has it help me?

_____

_____

_____

_____

_____

_____

Consistency

Let us not become weary in doing good, for at the proper time we will reap a harvest if we do not give up. Galatians 6:9 (NIV)

The first thing you must see in this scripture is the promise of a harvest for those who do not give up. From time to time, you will get weary on the journey of life. You keep doing the right thing, yet it does not appear to be producing many results. Day in and day out you keep expecting a breakthrough, but it does not seem to be heading in your direction. You get weary in waiting and wonder if God will ever move. You keep looking for Him but do not see Him on the horizon. This used to be one of my favorite sayings, "God created the world in six days, what is taking Him so long to move in the areas of my life?" Admit it, some of you have also wondered about this yourself. I am here to tell you do not give up. He will show up, He will bring you through. He will do so without fail.

Consistency is one of the greatest keys and it will get you the results and the breakthroughs you are hoping for. The word 'consistency' suggests a picture of uniformity. It is the picture of one who goes about doing what is regular and routine. They do their regular du ties on a consistent basis. These duties do not change. They are a part of the routine that must be adhered to if things are going to be in sync and produce the proper results. In order to produce the results you are expecting, you must stay consistent and be determined. You must adapt yourself to what God is doing in your life and in your situation.

Consistency is one of the keys that will gain you a reward in the Kingdom of God and provide a blessing in the lives of those with whom you come into contact. When you consistently follow through and are faithful, people will be able to say, "They know you." They will know you are a person they can trust because you are consistent in your commitment to do what you say you will do. Choose to make consistency a part of your everyday life, then watch and see the many blessings that will flood your way.

What does consistency mean to me?

_____

_____

_____

_____

_____

_____

_____

Tenacity

Let us hold unswervingly to the hope we profess, for He who promised is faithful. Hebrews 10:23 (NIV)

So do not throw away your confidence; it will be richly rewarded. You need to per severe so that when you have done the will of God, you will receive what He has promised. Hebrews 10:35 – 36 (NIV)

Most of you have heard the term "bulldog tenacity." This term is a picture of what it means to be tenacious. The bulldog is a stocky dog with short sturdy limbs. Their temperament is generally docile, friendly, and gregarious. They are fiercely loyal and can occasionally be willful. Bulldogs are very attached to their families and their homes, and they will not venture out alone without a companion. They are extremely intelligent, can be ferocious and will viciously attack a person, if they feel threatened. If they manage to take hold of whoever provoked them, they will not let go. They have a great deal of courage and can be very stubborn. You must develop this attitude as it relates to the enemy's attack in your life. He comes to steal your joy, health, wealth, and your family. Like the bulldog, you must become vicious and be ferocious against the damage the enemy intends to bring against you. You cannot afford to sit back and allow him to keep you from God's plan for your life.

The scriptures tell us to give no place to the devil (Ephesians 4:27). Do not give him a foothold to bring his deception and lies into your life and relationships. Have the courage to stand against all the attacks he attempts to bring to your mind. Remember to take every thought captive and subject it to the leadership of the Holy Spirit. It will take courage for you to stand up in the face of adversity, to draw a line in the sand, and to tell the devil he will proceed no further in his destruction of your life. Tenacity is an important key because it keeps you in the fight. It keeps you from giving up when the battles are raging out of control. It gives you the determination to be steadfast no matter what you face, and to declare that the Lord is good, and to know He is fighting these battles for you.

In what areas do I need to be more tenacious?

_____

_____

_____

_____

_____

_____

_____

_____

_____

A Prayer for Endurance

Father, in the name of Jesus, I am truly in need of Your help. The battles have been out of control in my life, and I am not sure of what to do and how to hold on. In Jesus' name, I pray the Holy Spirit will give me the grace to stand, and having done all, to stand as long as it takes to win. I have determined in my heart that Your intention is always for me to win in every battle, and I ask You to reveal to me the strategies for winning. I will discipline myself and submit my body and will over to Your control and Your instruction. I commit to be consistent with my prayer life and seek Your face regularly for the answers that only You can provide. You promise to open the windows of heaven and to pour out blessings that I will not have room enough to receive. One of your blessings is the ability to be steadfast and immovable during every trial.

Remind me that Your Word declares I am the head and not the tail, and I am above and not beneath. I am the victor in every battle because You have already won them all for me. Re mind me that Your goodness and mercy follow me all the days of my life, so it is impossible for me to be alone in the battles. Father, in Jesus' name, give me the tenacity and stamina to stand and keep on standing, to believe and keep on believing, and to be steady no matter where the winds of life may take me. I am resting and depending on You as Daniel did. I know You will answer me as You answered him because You are no respecter of persons. I ask You to keep me under the shelter of Your protection in Jesus' name. Thank You, Father, that every time I pray You hear me, and the answers are on the way. I win in Jesus' name! Amen!

You will face and overcome the battles!

What Battle?
Chapter 3

Do you have a clear understanding that you are a winner? Do you fully realize God is on your side and it is impossible for you to lose in any battle you face? Since you win, let us talk about the battles and struggles many of you have encountered or are currently facing. I pose the question, "What battle?" because many of you are going through some devastating times and may not fully understand what you are in or just what is coming against you. The battles you are facing are often called "spiritual warfare." Spiritual warfare is Satan's hostilities against the people of God. He is antagonizing you and opposing you at every turn. He is acting belligerently because he knows God is on your side; he wants to separate you from Him. Satan knows God is a force to be reckoned with as he comes against you, so he tries to be subtle in his attacks. Satan has taken a warlike position against you because he is determined to keep you from winning and overcoming the battles of life. He is your enemy, a liar and he wants you to believe you will not overcome and be victorious. I want you to know today no matter how hostile he is, or how much he opposes you; he cannot win because he has already been defeated. Jesus defeated him once and for all on Calvary, so Satan has put up a smoke screen to keep you from seeing he is powerless to cause you permanent harm. He is living in a place of defeat.

There has been open war between the Kingdom of God and the devil's kingdom since he was kicked out of heaven. This war has been raging over God's people and their position with God. Satan wants worship so he causes situations to happen in your life to get you to focus on the circumstances and take your eyes off God who has the solutions. He is out to gain a place in your life because he lost his position in heaven. Satan's plan of operation since the beginning of time, as we know it, has been to invade the lives of believers. He is on a campaign for the souls of men, and his intention is to destroy believers. He does not care how often you go to church or how much you worship God, because he stages situations to try and get you off track even in the midst of your walk of faith. But it does not matter what Satan plots or what he does; you have the victory! Jesus defeated him and gave you victory over him and his demons.

Most of the attacks you encounter will be waged against your mind because it is the control center for your life. If the devil can take control of one small area of your mind, then he can move to other weakened areas of your life in his quest to 'try' and dominate you. The key word in this sentence is "try." Understand Satan will try but he cannot win unless you give him permission.

Listen to this scripture *"Be strong in the Lord and in his mighty power. Put on the full armor of God so you can take your stand against the devil's schemes. For our struggle is not against flesh and blood, but against the rulers, against the authorities, against the powers of this dark world and against the spiritual forces of evil in the heavenly realms." Ephesians 6:10 –12 (NIV).*

You are in a struggle and are wrestling against spiritual forces; these are demons that serve the devil. The Apostle Paul, during the first century, gives us a clear picture of what this fight looks like. When a person is in a struggle, wrestling, or in hand-to-hand combat, it is a personal fight. In the battles you face, the fight is between you and the devil and no one else. The scripture says the battle is against powers, authorities, rulers, principalities, and spiritual forces that live in the heavenly realm. Who are these forces that have engaged you in warfare? Read on as we explore their origin and their assignments.

What battles am I fighting and how strong am I?

_____

_____

_____

_____

_____

_____

_____

_____

_____

_____

_____

_____

_____

_____

_____

_____

_____

_____

_____

Principalities

Satan has no original idea or thought in his head. He is a deceiver and has tried to copy what God has established in heaven. The term 'principalities' was first used in heaven to describe the order of the angelic hosts assigned to minister to God's people. The word now refers to demons in the devil's kingdom. God's angels are assigned as caretakers over nations, provinces, countries, districts, cities, towns, and villages. They are God's administrators and have direct access into the affairs of humanity. God has given them power and ability to move the hearts of men and women to help us receive all God has provided for our lives.

It is, therefore, not surprising the devil has set up his kingdom using the same hierarchy. The devil assigns his minions to kill, steal and destroy the exact opposite of what God does to His people. In the devil's kingdom, principalities are the highest level of demons. Although they have been given a high, lofty position, and are often considered the leaders, the chiefs, or the heads of their organizations, they have limited and temporary power. These spirits are assigned to bring chaos and confusion into cities, nations, provinces, and to churches, as well as other Christian organizations. Their assignment is to destroy what has been established in, and for, the name of the Lord.

Because Satan robbed Adam and Eve of their authority and dominion, we now live within a system that is filled with moral and social decay. These principalities are assigned by Satan to help carry out destruction and moral decay upon the earth. It is in direct opposition to what God intended. God's desire is for you to have a heart that pleases Him by doing what He has established. Please know with certainty, as we explore the other demonic assignments, that you have the power of the Holy Spirit residing in you. He ensures your victory because His power is at work in you. He is more powerful than the devil and all his demon forces combined. The Godhead has commissioned His angels to protect the heirs of salvation – this makes us winners and more than conquerors in any battle!

How am I walking in the authority that God has given me over the enemy?

_____
_____
_____
_____
_____
_____
_____
_____

Authorities/Powers

In the hierarchy of the devil's kingdom, authorities and powers have the second level of governmental rule. They are demonic spirits that control a world that is in rebellion to God. These spirits have been given delegated authority that was stolen from Adam and Eve. They use their authority to bring destruction into people's lives and attempt to sabotage the plans God has put in place for your ultimate victory. They administrate the plans and strategies of the devil. They attack people's thinking and ultimately their decisions and use the power of influence to get many of you off the right path to going down the wrong path.

These powers attempt to influence your thoughts, which then influence your attitude and affect your actions. Often, they will control your thoughts and mastermind their action plan into your mind. The goal of the enemies of God and His children is to hold tightly onto you. If they succeed, they will grip you so securely eventually you will feel as if you are bound forever. The devil attempts to sink his fangs into your mind where he does battle for your soul, and he is a like an octopus once he gets a hold of you. He endeavors to use his power with force to steamroll you into believing you are unable to be free. What he does not seem to comprehend, even after being in existence for thousands of years, is whom the Son sets free is free indeed!   As we are told by James, the Lord's brother in James 4:7 (NIV) – *"Submit yourselves, then, to God. Resist the devil, and He will flee from you."* You have a greater power given to you by God in the presence of the Holy Spirit who lives in you. The Holy Spirit governs your life and gives you the might, the determination, and the ability to win every single attack the enemy brings against you.

How has the enemy attempted to influence my thoughts and attitude?

_____

_____

_____

_____

_____

_____

_____

_____

_____

Rulers

Rulers are spirits who appear third in the order of the devil's kingdom. They are spirits that have power and position in the devil's order of service. They have been trained for battle the same way we train our military officers to go to war against our enemies. These rulers follow a set plan of action by their leader, are assigned tasks, and are given strategies that they follow to the letter. They stay in formation and often war together.

In Matthew twelve, Jesus told the story of what happens when we operate in unbelief. He talked to the Pharisees about desiring a sign and not believing He was greater than all previous prophets. He told them a greater one than Solomon was among them and shared this story with them. *"When an unclean spirit comes out of a man, he roams through dry places, looking for rest but doesn't find any. Then it says, I will go back to my house that I came from and when it arrives, it finds the house vacant and swept, and put in order. Then off it goes and brings with it seven other spirits more evil than itself, and they enter and settle down there. As a result, that man's last condition is worse than the first."* (Matt. 12:4345). He shared this story with them to paint a clear picture of what would happen to an evil generation. These rulers only have temporary mastery over those they have been assigned to attack and destroy. They act as overlords but also take their orders from the devil who has them on strings, like puppets. But they are determined to succeed. It is clear from this pas sage, in his attempts to destroy you, the devil and his rulers will get help to bring further destruction. Be sure your house (heart) is never empty but filled with the power and presence of God. Fill your heart daily with the Word of God, taking His word as medicine to your soul. Give no place in your heart to the devil or to his rulers. Do not allow them to bring destruction to your life. You have the power and authority to ensure that every empty place is filled with God this leaves no room for the devil and his demons to enter or inhabit your life.

What am I doing to keep my heart pure?

_____
_____
_____
_____
_____
_____
_____
_____
_____
_____

Spiritual Forces

Spiritual forces appear at the fourth level in the devil's kingdom. The Bible describes them as forces of evil in the heavenly realm. They are an army of wicked spirits who battle in the spiritual realm. They act by compulsion, and their tactics are to coerce you into believing you cannot win. They are combative and will use their strength against you, acting as assailants who have been assigned to do extreme damage to your mind, and ultimately, to your heart. These forces are belligerent and are determined to gain control and mastery over your thoughts, your life, and your actions; but in all their attempts to bring you down, you are still mightier than they are. You have more power available to you than all of them combined. The Greater One lives in you and has already ensured your victory. You have an unlimited supply of overcoming power that you can tap into. Decide that you will fill your heart with God's Word and His Presence and live a life filled with the discipline of the Holy Spirit. When you set your heart to know and follow God, you will be armed and dangerous to the devil because each time he approaches with his lies and condemnation, you can remind him of who you are and whose you are. You are the righteousness of God in Christ Jesus and you overcome him by the blood of the Lamb and the word of your testimony. Your testimony is found in 1 John 4:4 and says, "Greater is He that is in you than he that is in the world." You have power to overcome, power to conqueror, and power to succeed to live a victorious life. God loves you and gives His all to ensure your redemption and your success, and He gives you power to win in every battle.

How has the power of the Holy Spirit been effective in my life to combat the enemy's attacks?

_____

_____

_____

_____

_____

_____

_____

_____

_____

Who engages you in the fight?

There is a real enemy who engages you in the battles you are facing. The book of Isaiah records the story of the devil's fall from heaven and from grace. He was a beautiful being who led praise and worship for God in heaven. One day he decided he wanted to be like the Most High God. He desired to be worshipped, praised, and adored. His pride and lofty desires caused him to be thrown out of heaven with one third of the angels who also rebelled with him (Isaiah 14:12-20).

When God created you, you took the devil's place in worshipping the Most High God along with the remaining angels in heaven. Therefore believers often face so many challenges when they open their mouths and begin to praise and worship God. You may experience some distractions the moment you decide to lift your heart and voice in worship to God. The devil desires to keep you focused on the situations around you to keep you from being able to press fully into God's presence and give Him the praise and worship He so richly deserves.

Because the devil wanted the worship in heaven that he was denied, he has found a way to get his worship from you. Difficulties, hardship, sickness, disease, etc. come into your life to distract you and you can worry and complain about them. Whenever you begin to murmur and complain about your difficulties and are unhappy and dissatisfied with your life, you inadvertently pay homage to the devil. Murmuring and complaining give him the worship he is seeking. It keeps your focus off God and places it on the difficulties you are enduring. When you are focused on those difficulties you lose hope and confidence in God's ability to bring you through. You will then begin to worry and fret, which leads to further complaining and indicates you do not trust that God can handle your situation and bring deliverance to you. There is only One who deserves to be worshipped so decide not to give the devil any satisfaction by worrying and complaining. Our deliverance will come not so much from trying but from simply trusting that God has you in His hands and nothing and no one can pluck you out of them (John 10:28). He will truly, truly perfect that which concerns you.

What difficulties cause me to murmur and complain?

_____
_____
_____
_____
_____
_____
_____
_____
_____
_____

Prayer of Protection

Father, in the name of Jesus, I acknowledge I am in a battle that is staged by the devil to defeat me; but because of Jesus and the power of the Holy Spirit in me, I win. I ask You, Father, to give me wisdom each day to know the strategies of the enemy and to know that with You all things are possible to me. Keep me from being fearful and from being intimidated. Help me to know You are in control and I can trust You to see me through. Father, give me the grace to trust You and not to worry and complain. It is not my desire to worship or honor the devil in any way, and I will not honor him by worrying and complaining. Father, I choose to trust and to seek You for guidance on a daily basis. Thank You that Your Word says one can put a thousand to flight but two can put ten thousand to flight. You are with me, and I am more than a conqueror.

I understand I am a soldier in the army of God, and I must discipline myself by praying and studying Your Word so I will not lose or fail. With the Holy Spirit's help, I will stand and be ready to face my difficulties because I am assured of His presence and His power. In Psalm 91 You promise to give Your angels charge over me and I accept that promise today. You are mightier than all the forces of darkness and it is to You I run for safety and protection.

Thank You, Father, for watching over my life and for perfecting everything that concerns me, in Jesus' name. You are my Abba (Father) and I trust You.

Amen!

Standing Firm in the Battles
Chapter 4

There are various stages in each battle you will face, and each stage has steps you must follow. To win, you must recognize there is a spiritual enemy. 1 Peter 5:89 says to be sober (alert), be vigilant because your adversary the devil walks about like a roaring lion seeking whom he may devour. This scripture gives you the ingredients that are necessary to make a bold stand against the devil.

Recognize

A major ingredient while standing is to recognize, as well as acknowledge, the devil is on the prowl, and his intention is to conquer and to devour. He has lived for centuries and knows every trick in the book, and he uses them effectively because he is determined to win. Remember, in the beginning he was with Adam and Eve. He managed to deceive Eve into questioning the instructions God had given to her husband and consequently to her. He is always lurking. It is evident he must have been in the Garden of Eden when Adam told Eve not to eat from that one tree in the garden. When he approached Eve, he repeated to her almost exactly what God had said to Adam, which signifies he was listening in on their conversation. He found a kink in her story because she added to the instructions. God never told Adam not to touch the tree, He only told him not to eat from it. I am sure, when the devil heard her rendition of the story, he realized she had not received the instructions clearly, so he went in to kill and to destroy them. It is paramount you not only perceive who the devil is, but also realize he uses many tactics to get his job done. He caused Eve to doubt her hearing and understanding. You must be sober, alert, and aware, and always be on the look out to recognize his attacks and counter attacks. He is prowling around as a lion seeking whom he may devour.

In what ways has the enemy caused me to doubt what I am hearing from God?

_____

_____

_____

_____

_____

_____

_____

_____

_____

Repent

Now that you recognize your adversary, the devil, and know he comes to kill and destroy you, beware his goal is to keep you in a cycle of sin and sinning. It is necessary to close every door that once was opened to him. Some have opened doors and were not fully aware these opened doors were giving him access into their lives. Things that seemed fun at one time such as palm reading, horoscope, witchcraft activities, the psychic hotlines, movies, and books that deal with the demonic realms, are doors he has used to gain entry into many lives. He caused many to believe they were obtaining knowledge they did not already have. He can only tell you about your past and what is presently happening to you, but he most certainly does not know the future and cannot predict it.

Repent means to turn around. It is a picture of going in the wrong direction, then making a one hundred and eighty degree turn and going in the exact opposite direction from where you were headed. Repent also means to run away from. When sin comes knocking, don't open the door and let it in. Decide today sin is not for you, and that living in sin is not what you want. Decide you will not do anything displeasing to God. One of my daily prayers is asking God to help me not do anything that would bring shame to His Name and His Kingdom. Every time sin is presented to you by the devil, turn aside from it and embrace the life God has reserved for you. The enemy will try his best to bombard your mind with all types of sins and enticements, but you have power to say "no" and to mean "no". You cannot vacillate in your decision to stand for what is right and good for your life. 1 John 1:9 says, if you confess your sins, He is faithful and just to forgive you and to cleanse you from all unrighteousness.

What sins do I need to repent for and turn away from?

_____

_____

_____

_____

_____

_____

_____

_____

_____

_____

_____

_____

Resist

The word "resist" is a strong and decisive word, and this is your position when you take a stand against the devil's attacks in your life. Be strong and decisive as you resist the devil's attempts to invade your life and bring chaos. In resisting the enemy, you are opposing him and withstanding his attempts to keep you in a cycle of pain, lack, sickness, and disease – your destruction. The word 'resist' also suggests there is a struggle going on in your mind. This struggle is against the unwholesome, negative, critical, and destructive thoughts the enemy attempts to deposit in your mind causing you to react and act.

He invades your mind by bombarding your thoughts with all his destructive plans. James 4:7 says, "Therefore submit to God. Resist the devil and he will flee from you." The scripture is clear you have a part to play for the devil to flee from your life. You must submit all your desires, plans, hopes, and dreams to God. Submission requires a surrendering of all you are so God can reign and rule in your heart and life. After submitting everything to God, you need to take it a step further. You must resist the devil and he will flee from you with his thoughts, plans, and harmful imaginations.

To resist means you will defend what is yours. You will defend your peace of mind, goals, dreams, family, and finances; and you will let the devil know there is a "No trespassing sign" attached to your life. Resisting means you must be willing to fight and persevere. You will fight the lies the devil attempts to plant in the soil of your mind. When you are submitted to God, you then have the power to resist the devil and he must flee from you.

In what ways do I resist the devil?

_____

_____

_____

_____

_____

_____

_____

_____

_____

_____

_____

_____

Replace

After you have recognized the enemy's strategies and have repented of all your wrong thoughts and wrong actions, then learn to resist his attempts to draw you back into a life of sin and shame. To succeed, you must replace all the unwholesome thoughts and actions of your past with what God has done in your life. The devil plants his thoughts into your mind so he can get a foothold in your life. He will then lead you like a dog on a leash straight back into the devastation he intends for you.

But God! Why don't you say it "**But God!**" But God has given you His assurance in Revelation 12:11 which tells us they overcame him (devil) by the blood of the Lamb and by the word of their testimony, and they did not love their lives so much as to shrink from death. The word "replace" suggests something or someone has been removed or taken from you, and that something or someone else needs to be put back into its place. Refuse to let the enemy steal your soundness of mind, joy, hope, peace, and the ability to love freely. Replace all the devil's lies, distortion of the truth, his thoughts, and his imaginations with the truth of God's Word. To fill your life again with truth, replace the seeds that have taken root in your heart and those which have begun to bear the wrong type of fruit in your life, with the Word.

Each time you discover a fruit in your life that is unpleasant, and you know it is not what God has in mind for you, substitute it by planting positive seeds of the Word of God into the same soil. As you make deposits of the Word, which is the right seed in good soil, you will begin to experience the right kind of harvest in your life. Ask the Lord to restore everything the enemy has stolen from you. Know you have the authority to make a demand on His Word and to receive kingdom blessings.

When a thief steals from you, if he is caught, he must repay sevenfold even if it costs him all the wealth of his house (Prov. 6:3031). The devil is a thief, and he is commanded to pay back a sevenfold return of everything he has stolen from you. Has the enemy robbed you of a spouse? Has he robbed you of your health? Then he must return to you sevenfold which means seven times better than what you had – he must obey the Lord and return it to you, in Jesus' name! Declare and claim it because it is the promise of the Lord to believers.

Jesus, who was without sin, had no need to repent; but He had to recognize the devil's lies and distortions of the truth of the Word. He resisted temptation and won, even though He was tested and tempted as we are. He, too, had to replace the devil's lies with the truth of God's Word; and in doing so, He showed us how to overcome. Jesus knew the Word of God. He allowed the Word of God to take center stage in His life. He meditated on it day and night, so when the enemy came to distort the Word, He could not deceive Jesus who had the truth and knowledge of the Word in Him. The enemy cannot win over you if you make the Word of God central in your life. When you meditate on the Word day and night, and engrave it in your heart, it will be impossible for the devil to lie to you and cause you to fail to live righteously before God.

What thoughts need replacing in my life?

_____

_____

_____

_____

_____

_____

_____

Weapons of Warfare
The Truth of God's Word

To the Jews who had believed Him, Jesus said, "If you hold to my teaching, you are really my disciples. Then you will know the truth, and the truth will set you free." John 8:3132 (NIV)

The truth of the Word of God is the most effective weapon against an attack of the enemy. When you embrace the teachings of Jesus and begin applying the principles that He teaches, the scripture says then you will really be His disciples. To really be His means you are for Him, in Him, and living the life He gave you access to. You are His indeed! As you apply the truth of the Word of God to your life, the truth begins to permeate every area of your life. It takes over and is present in every decision you make, in what you choose to do, and how you choose to live. Truth becomes the fabric of who you are because you are aware that, as the truth is present in your life, God is present. The truth of God's Word begins to shape the way you act and react to situations. As you embrace the truth, the truth that you know and understand and apply it to your life's circumstances, it will set you free. This freedom will bring glory and honor to God in whatever situation you encounter.

What is my relationship with God's Word?

_____

_____

_____

_____

_____

_____

Righteousness

The Lord has also given you His righteousness as another weapon to use against the enemy. He has given you right standing and made you an upright, moral, and just person. As you choose righteousness, the enemy knows you will do what is right and pleasing in the eyes of the Lord. Each time he comes and entices you into doing wrong, your righteous stance will warn him to find someone else with whom to play his games of destruction. He will see written on your heart a sign that clearly says, "Righteousness lives here – no trespassing."

What does it mean to me to be righteous?

_____

_____

_____

_____

_____

_____

_____

Peace

Peace – say it "peace." Just saying the word calms your soul. God has given every believer the ability to have peace in all situations. When the devil brings his attacks against you, his desire is to move you from your position of peace into a place of unrest. In this place of unrest, he can get your focus off the truth and on thoughts that will traumatize you. The enemy may thrust you into trials to rob you of your peace and cause you to doubt God's sufficiency; but, as you stay connected to the source of peace, Jesus, our Prince of Peace, you will remain calm no matter what is going on around you. John 10:10 (NIV) says, "*The thief comes only to steal, and kill and destroy; I have come that they may have life and have it to the full.*" He is a thief who wants to steal your peace of mind. Peace is vital to your success in the battle so never let go of this weapon.

How does God's peace work in my life?

_____

_____

_____

_____

_____

_____

Salvation

Remembering God has provided salvation for you through His beloved Son is another great weapon against the devil. Salvation not only means to save but it also means to deliver. As you remind yourself of the great salvation Jesus provided, you can be confident that what you are currently facing will eventually pass. Everything you encounter in life comes to pass. It does not come to stay. Life is a cycle and everything that comes against you will eventually pass away. The devil wants you to believe the challenges you are facing will become permanent fixtures in your life and you will never get out from under them, but he is a deceiver. The saving grace of Jesus provides you a way of escape in every trial you face. Salvation brings you strength in the midst of the storms; salvation brings you hope in the midst of hopeless situations; and salvation is your place of safety when life gets difficult. The salvation from the finished work of Jesus on the cross has paid the ultimate price for our freedom.

What is my salvation experience?

_____

_____

_____

_____

_____

_____

_____

_____

_____

Meditation

As you meditate daily on the Word of God, your heart is impacted with the weapon that will cause the devil to pull back and leave you alone. In Joshua 1:8 (NIV), the Bible gives a strong encouragement. It says, "*Do not let this Book of the Law depart from your mouth; meditate on it day and night, so that you may be careful to do everything written in it. Then you will be prosperous and successful.*" To meditate means to constantly think of and to mutter over and over. To meditate on God's Word means you must train yourself to think on the things of God over and over again. It takes practice but meditating on what God has said as opposed to meditating over the lies of the devil is a powerful tool in your arsenal of weapons.

What things do I consistently meditate on?

_____

_____

_____

_____

_____

_____

_____

_____

_____

The Need for Prayer

Prayer is probably the greatest, most powerful weapon you have; and it causes severe dam age to the devil's kingdom. When you choose to lift your voice to the only true Source of help, the enemy cannot stand. Prayer releases power to change your situation. Every time you pray, God activates the angels to go to war on your behalf. Praying demonstrates you are determined to win, and you have aligned yourself with God by using one of His greatest weapons at your disposal, which guarantees your success. The Bible says, 'pray without ceasing'. This means to have a prayerful heart by always thinking about God and His goodness. Focus on His greatness and the fact He cannot and will not fail. Bathe yourself and your loved ones in prayer daily; then watch the effect of this weapon. Each time you pray, you send him running away from you instead of bringing his troubles to you. Prayer deflects the devil's attacks from you because He understands each time he attacks you, you go to your Father and your Father stands and fights for you.

How often do I pray and what things do I pray for?

_____

_____

_____

_____

_____

_____

_____

_____

_____

_____

The Blood of the Lamb

The final weapon we will cover in this chapter is the blood of the Lamb and the word of our testimony. The Bible says we overcome the devil by the blood of the Lamb and the word of our testimony (Rev. 12:11). Your overcoming testimony is to repeat what God has so clearly said about you in His Word. It is where you were when He found you and brought His saving grace into your life. The blood of the Lamb has power to change your mind, your life and all the circumstances you face.

Moses slaughtered the ram and took some of its blood and put it on the lobe of Aaron's right ear, on the thumb of his right hand and on the big toe of his right foot. Moses also brought Aaron's sons forward and put some of the blood on the lobes of their right ears, on the thumbs of their right hands and on the big toes of their right feet. Then he sprinkled blood against the altar on all sides. Leviticus 8:23-24 (NIV)

In this passage, God commanded Moses to consecrate Aaron and his sons to serve as priests in the house of the Lord. Moses prayed and consecrated everything in the temple in preparation for what God asked him to do. He took anointing oil and anointed everything in the temple and poured the anointing oil on Aaron's head to anoint and consecrate him to the Lord. Then Moses killed a ram and did something interesting with it. After killing the ram, he sprinkled the blood against the altar. He then dipped his finger into the blood of the ram and applied it to Aaron's right ear to consecrate his ear to hear and follow only the voice of God. He then applied the blood to the right thumb of Aaron's hand and consecrated his hands to be used in service to God. Finally, Moses dipped his finger in the blood again, and this time, he applied the blood to the big toe of Aaron's right foot thus consecrating his feet to always bring the gospel of peace to the people of God. Then Moses consecrated Aaron's sons in the same manner.

My point in sharing this story is Moses understood there was power in the blood. The ram's blood did not have power in itself; but when faith, prayer, and God were a part of the equation, the blood had power to change lives. You have been given the blood of Jesus as one of your greatest weapons. His blood has the power to change and transform your life and every circumstance. Since Moses understood a ram's blood could be used to consecrate people in service to God, then you and I must understand the blood of Jesus can consecrate us in service to God, as well. When the enemy tries to attack you, remember the blood. There is pow er in the blood to change you and others around you. When you apply the blood of Jesus to your life, you safeguard your mind against an attack from the enemy.

What has the blood of Jesus accomplished for me and what does it mean for my life?

_____

_____

_____

_____

_____

_____

_____

_____

Prayer for Standing Firm

Father, in the name of Jesus I ask You to teach me how to stand and to stand firm in each difficult situation I face. The Word tells me to be steadfast, immovable, always abounding in the works of the Lord for I know that my labor is not in vain in the Lord. Father, please help me to be steady in the storms of life. Help me to not be moved from my position of trust and confidence in You. Help me to know I can do all things through Christ who strengthens me. As I recognize the strategies of the enemy, help me Lord to resist these attempts to get me off course and onto the wrong path. Lord, I repent for anytime I have listened to his lies and missed hearing Your voice and feeling Your comfort in the storms I have faced. I choose to replace all the lies he has told me with the truth of Your Word. I will use the weapons You have provided for me to firmly stand and win the war.

I trust in Your Word and Your promises that You will be faithful to perform. As I daily clothe myself in Your righteousness, I know that I am covered in the precious blood of Jesus, and because of all He sacrificed for me I have complete peace and assurance in His presence. Help me Lord to remember I cannot fail because You have won the victory for me at Calvary. Thanks so much for loving me and for giving me a firm foundation on which to stand. My firm foundation is on the solid rock of Your Son, Jesus Christ. Thank You, Father, for Your amazing love for me, in Jesus' name.

Amen!

Personal Notes/Reflection

Overcoming
the
traps
of the
enemy!

Self-Sufficiency Trap
Chapter 5

All of us at some point in our lives have fallen into a trap that was staged for our downfall. These traps were set by the enemy and were designed to keep us from moving forward and from accomplishing the goals that were put in place for our lives. As a believer, be aware the enemy has designed an outcome for you that is far different from the great destiny God has planned for your life. He has set up strategic traps to keep you in fear and bondage. You have power with the help of the Holy Spirit to overcome and be victorious over each of these traps. The enemy cannot hold you down, keep you back or restrain you from having the victory and from becoming a winner. In this chapter we will explore some of the many traps that have been staged for your downfall. We will talk about the self-sufficiency trap, disobedience trap, mind trap, mouth trap, sin trap, poverty mentality trap, and the approval trap. Are you ready to explore these traps and to find the keys for your victory over them? If you are, open your heart and ask the Holy Spirit to show you which of these traps has kept you in bondage and kept you from His best plan for your life.

I am the true vine, and my Father is the gardener. He cuts off every branch in me that bears no fruit, while every branch that does bear fruit he prunes so that it will be even more fruitful. You are already clean because of the word I have spoken to you. Remain in me, and I will remain in you. No branch can bear fruit by itself; it must remain in the vine. Neither can you bear fruit unless you remain in me. John 15:14 (NIV)

It is a trap of the enemy to believe you are self-sufficient needing no one including God. God did not design you to be fully satisfied or to be complete by finding sufficiency only in yourself. God designed you to be interconnected to Him and with the need to develop and experience fulfillment in earthly relationships. We need to have horizontal relationships with our family, friends, and associates as well as a vertical relationship with God, our heavenly Father. The cross of Jesus gives us a great picture of what this relationship looks like. In the center of the cross is a vertical piece that points us to heaven and to God, our helper, and there are two horizontal pieces, which signify outstretched arms to embrace mankind. When Jesus hung on the cross, His head was pointed to heaven while His arms were outstretched to man. This is a picture of what your life should be like. You need the Lord to be the head of your life to lead, govern, and guide you. At the same time, you need relationships with others who can mentor you in your growth and development, and who can help you, as you face and overcome the struggles of life. God did not intend for you to be alone. You need people to fulfill your needs, as well as to help you in your day-to-day existence.

Letting go of self-sufficiency brings:

- An understanding that you cannot live without God and others. When you acknowledge this your life will abound with blessings, favor and the many gifts God has reserved for you.

- An acceptance of the need for God and a realization of His faithfulness in your life.

- The Realization of who He is. One day I came to the realization of how totally dependent I am on God and how desperately I need Him for every detail in my life.

- Acknowledgment it is God who gives you the breath to live, and without His decision to give you a new day there would be no life in you.

- An understanding God is the one who determines you still have a purpose in the earth realm, a reason to have life, and His breath for a new day.

- Gratefulness you have another day to fulfill what He has mapped out for your life.

- Acknowledgement God is your all sufficiency; and as you stay connected to Him, you will grow and develop, and be able to soar over the battles you face.

- The ability to abide in God, which gives you the power and knowledge that He will meet all your needs according to His riches in Glory by Christ Jesus (Phil. 4:19).

There is no need for you to attempt to be self-sufficient because Jesus' arms are outstretched toward you with an abundant supply of provisions and blessings.

How have I operated in self-sufficiency?

_____

_____

_____

_____

_____

_____

_____

_____

_____

_____

_____

Personal Notes/Reflection

Disobedience Trap
Chapter 6

The Word of the Lord came to Jonah son of Amittai. "Go to the great city of Nineveh and preach against it, because its wickedness has come up before me." But Jonah ran away from the Lord and headed for Tarshish. He went down to Joppa, where he found a ship bound for that port. After paying the fare, he went aboard and sailed for Tarshish to flee from the Lord. Then the Lord sent a great wind on the sea, and such a violent storm arose that the ship threatened to break up. All the sailors were afraid and each cried out to his god. And they threw the cargo into the sea to lighten the ship. But Jonah had gone below deck, where he lay down and fell into a deep sleep. Jonah 1:15 (NIV)

Disobedience is one of the enemy's most deadly traps because it will keep you from a true intimate relationship with God. Disobedience will cause you to miss out on the blessings God has for your life because God is not able to approve or bless what you are doing. Disobedience will also cause you to make some bad and harmful choices that will produce dire consequences in your life. It will keep you feeling guilty and away from the presence of God. Think about a time in your life when you were walking in disobedience. Did you feel a strong desire to pray? Were you excited to get into God's presence? Were you able to freely talk with Him about your concerns? Did you find yourself drifting further and further away from Him? One small act of disobedience will cause you to drift away from God to such a degree it is often difficult for you to find your way back to Him.

God gave Jonah an assignment to go to Nineveh because the sins of the people had become repugnant to Him. Before He brought destruction on them, He wanted to warn them and give them an opportunity to repent and turn back to Him. Jonah disobeyed the assignment the Lord gave him. Since Jonah had intimate knowledge of God, I believe he knew if he went to the Ninevites and told them what God said and they repented, God would change His mind and spare their lives. I am sure Jonah felt the trip would be a waste of his time and effort, so he disobeyed God and boarded a ship that was headed in another direction. Jonah chose disobedience over God's instructions by trying to run away from God. A storm arose. Storms will always arise in the midst of your disobedience. The sailors were concerned for their lives and began to pray to their individual gods for help.

Jonah finally repented and walked away from his disobedience and followed through on God's instructions. He cried out to the Lord in prayer. "In my distress I called to the Lord, and He answered me. From the depths of the grave I called for help, and You listened to my cry. "Jonah finally understood what he was assigned to do was vital, and he had no choice but to obey. He also came to the realization that salvation could be found in no other person but God. When he realized and acknowledged the power of God to reach into the depth of his sin and lift him out, he finally surrendered; and God allowed the fish to vomit him out on dry land.

The Word of the Lord came a second time to Jonah and this time he obeyed. He could no longer run. There was no place where he could hide from God. Psalm 139:710 (NIV) says, "*Where can I go from your Spirit? Where can I flee from your presence? If I go up to the heavens, you are there; if I make my bed in the depths, you are there. If I rise on the wings of the dawn, if I settle on the far side of the sea, even there your hand will guide me, your right hand will hold me fast.*" Jonah discovered there was no place he could go to hide from God where His presence does not already exist. He realized God would always find and bring him back because God's purpose for his life and the lives of His people had to be fulfilled. You and I must embrace the same truth. In our disobedience, there is no place where we can hide from God because He will search for us, find us, and then draw us back to Himself so we can fulfill the purposes He has assigned for our lives.

After he was deposited on dry land by the fish, Jonah made his way to Nineveh and began to prophesy just as the Lord had commanded him. He told them God was going to destroy them because of their sins. The people heard the word of the prophet and repented sincerely and humbly before God. When the news reached the king of the Ninevites, he came off his throne, took off his royal robes, dressed himself in sackcloth and sat down in the dust in true repentance. The king made a decree that no man or beast was to eat anything, but all were to humble themselves and call urgently on God. He commanded them to give up their evil ways and their violence in the hope God would relent, have compassion, and turn His fierce anger from them so they would not perish (Jonah 3). And, just as Jonah had sensed in his heart, God forgave them and spared their lives. Now you would think Jonah would be happy with this outcome, but he was not. After God spared the Ninevites, Jonah became so angry with God he declared, "He was angry enough to die." The prophet was not happy with God's compassion or His deliverance of the people. It is evident he wanted them destroyed. God had to question him about his attitude. Disobedience can make us self-righteous and lacking the necessary compassion to rejoice when God has moved to change lives and to turn around peoples' horrible circumstances.

This is how Jonah's story ends in the Bible. Jonah sat down and began complaining against God. He said, "*Oh Lord, is this not what I said when I was still at home? That is why I was so quick to flee to Tarshish. I knew that You are a gracious and compassion ate God; slow to anger and abounding in love, a God who relents from sending calamity. Now, O Lord take away my life, for it is better for me to die than to live.*" (Jonah 4:23 NIV).

I challenge you not to let the story of your life be like the prophet Jonah's pouting and mad at God because of His goodness to others.

You can overcome this trap by choosing to:

- Obey God and trust that He knows best.

- Remember God will never lead you astray, nor will He lead you down a wrong path for
  your life.

- Understand this trap is designed to keep you from a deep intimate relationship with God.

- Choose not to get involved with the devil's schemes. 1 Samuel 15:22-23 says to obey is better than sacrifice. Obey God quickly; and, when you miss it, be quick to repent and ask for His pardon and forgiveness.

- Do not allow the devil to drive a wedge between you and God.

- Keep your relationship alive and thriving by choosing each day to obey His instructions and to follow His directives for your life.

I challenge you not to let the story of your life be like the prophet Jonah's.

How obedient am I to God? Site Examples.

_____
_____
_____
_____
_____
_____
_____
_____
_____
_____
_____
_____
_____
_____
_____

Personal Notes/Reflection

Mind Trap
Chapter 7

For though we live in the world, we do not wage war as the world does. The weapons we fight with are not the weapons of the world. On the contrary, they have divine power to demolish strongholds. We demolish arguments and every pretension that sets itself up against the knowledge of God, and we take captive every thought to make it obedient to Christ. 2 Corinthians 10:35 (NIV)

Are you experiencing turmoil in your mind? Are unholy and impure thoughts constantly running through your mind? There is a solution that provides a way of escape for you. This scripture tells us to take every thought captive and subject it under the leadership of Christ. It encourages you to align your thoughts with what God says about you. The mind trap is worth discussing because the enemy uses your mind as his battlefield. He plants seeds of doubt, lies, fear, accusation, and many other destructive thoughts in your mind. Since your mind is his battlefield, you will either win or lose the battles of life in your mind. You must learn to guard your mind and quickly take any ungodly thoughts and cast them down which lets the devil know you will not receive his lies.

You must also guard your mind so the enemy cannot build strongholds in your life. The word 'stronghold' is one of the oldest words in the New Testament and it is used to describe a fortress. A fortress is a high, thick wall that was designed to keep outsiders from getting in. In Greek the word means a prison. A prison keeps insiders from getting out. The Apostle Paul speaks of the types of strongholds the devil uses to keep you in turmoil. He uses lies and deceptions and plants them deeply into your belief system. Because these strongholds can become a part of your belief system, they are often very difficult to dislodge. Let us examine two examples of strongholds that the enemy uses against you.

What steps have I taken to guard my mind against the enemy's attacks?

_____

_____

_____

_____

_____

_____

_____

_____

Rational Strongholds

A rational stronghold makes sense to your mind. It is your imagination at work and is based on your reasoning. It is the logical part of your mind at work, and you often use sound judgment when making decisions. Therefore, since your rationalizing makes sense to you, you will delay obeying God and following His directions because what He is asking from you does not make sense.

A short time ago, I was scheduled to teach a Bible study class on a Thursday evening. As I began preparation for the class, I felt a strong urge to call the venue owner to see if all was ready for the class. I had previously taught eight sessions at this location, so there was no logical reason to call and verify everything was ready. Nevertheless, the desire to call persisted so I concluded this was a prompting from the Holy Spirit. I called the landlord to verify all was ready for the event and discovered he was having some challenges. It became apparent in our conversation the location would not be ready for the evening's study. I only had a few hours to find another location. The thought of canceling was at the forefront of my mind, but earlier that morning, in my prayer time, the Lord had told me five times to trust Him. At the time, I was not sure why He was so adamant about trusting Him. Later, I learned the reason. I called several people on the team, and we began a search to secure another location but were unsuccessful. In my rational thinking, it made sense to cancel the study and attach a note to the door of the location. Since I did not get clearance from the Holy Spirit to cancel, I proceeded with my preparation. Thirty minutes before I was ready to leave for the study, the landlord called to tell me the space would not be available that evening. I asked him to help me find a different location. He suggested we cancel and resume later but God had not given me those instructions. The Lord reminded him of a possible location, and within five minutes after making a call a new location was found and we proceeded.

The decision to proceed with the study was not rational. It would have made better sense to cancel, but God had another plan. His plan was what He told me that morning in prayer, "Trust Me."

What things has the Lord asked me to do that do not appear rational?

_____

_____

_____

_____

_____

_____

_____

Irrational Strongholds

An irrational stronghold is unrealistic fear and worry. There is nothing logical about your fears or worries. It is an abnormal fear of things that ninety nine percent of the time will never happen to you.

The lies the enemy plants in your mind are intended to sabotage your sense of self-worth and self-image. They are intended to insulate you from the truth and from people who can help you to clearly see the truth. There are invisible barriers that have surrounded your mind and heart and caused your emotions to be in turmoil. The enemy is attempting to keep you as a prisoner, and he is causing you to view life through the illusion of his lies. He has locked you in the prison of your mind, and you need to break free. He loves to make a playground out of your mind and your imagination, but you can defeat and overcome him by making yourself think thoughts that agree with God's will for your life.

Here is the challenge we all face. When we choose to meditate on the negative thoughts, we give those thoughts power over us. When the enemy plants the thoughts into your mind, he has no idea which of them you will believe and then act on. He is not all knowing – only God is. Throughout the day he plants thoughts, which are seeds, into your mind then he waits to see which of those thoughts you will activate. How do you activate these thoughts? They are activated by accepting them as your own and believing them, meditating on them, and then acting them out. He knows he has won when you speak out of your mouth the lying thought he planted in your mind, and you begin to act on it.

What lies has the enemy been telling me to keep me from God's best plan for my life?

_____

_____

_____

_____

_____

_____

_____

_____

_____

_____

_____

_____

_____

_____

To overcome this deadly trap:

- Find out how the devil is gaining a stronghold in your mind.

- When you discover which door is open to him, repent and ask God for His forgive ness, and then close the door in the devil's face.

- Make a decision to give him no further access to your life.

- Reject the enemy's lies about you on a daily basis.

- Choose to get back on the path to holiness by renewing your mind daily with the Word of God.

- Put a guard over you mind and mouth so you will not think on the negative thoughts, then they will not be spoken out of your mouth.

- Agree with what God's Word says about you and act out your agreement with His Word.

- Regularly cast down the vain imaginations that attack your mind.

- You must become violent against the enemy's attacks (Matt. 11:12).

- Become like Jesus and use the Word of God whenever you come under attack.

Personal Notes/Reflection

Mouth Trap
Chapter 8

I tell you the truth, if anyone says to this mountain, "Go throw yourself into the sea, and does not doubt in his heart but believes that what he says will happen, it will be done for him. Therefore I tell you, that whatever you ask for in prayer, believe that you have received it, and it will be yours. Mark 11:2324 (NIV)

Your mouth, tongue, and voice are all gifts from God. God has blessed you with these gifts so you can use them to glorify Him as well as bring blessings to your life. Your mouth can take you to the highest level in life, or to the lowest depth, because you truly will have what you say. Whatever you speak out of your mouth, whether good or bad is exactly what you will have. The key to having what you say is to have no doubt in your heart that what you say will come to pass. The word doubt means to hesitate, waiver, or differ. When your heart differs from what your mouth is saying, you will have what your mouth speaks.

Creative power is released when your heart and mouth agree. The unity between the heart and the mouth works together for the positive as well as for the negative. It is a proven fact that, when you speak something out of your mouth, those words are verified and empowered in your mind. When words take root in your mind and you process them by meditating on them, you bring life to those words. Eventually, they will be birthed when they are spoken out of your mouth. It is important to note when your mind is filled with the Word of God, those are the words that will come forth from you. The Word of God also strengthens your inner man, and you are not easily deceived. If you have not filled your heart and mind with the Word of God, you will encounter many situations you will not be able to rightly discern.

In Mark 11:2324, the message is clear about what you speak has the power to change situations and circumstances around you. Whatever trouble or battle you are facing is a mountain that can be moved with your spoken words. Your words have life and are powerful enough to demolish the mountains you are facing. As you pray without doubting, your words will not return to you empty. Those words will bring about the result you are seeking and will prosper wherever you send them (Isaiah 55:11). Your mouth can speak the truth in love and change the course of peoples' lives or you can use the same mouth to crucify them. Proverbs 18:21 says life and death are in the power of the tongue. You can use your mouth to speak life to your situation or you can use the same mouth to curse your life and miss out on what God has planned for you. There is a law of confession that goes like this— whatever you speak is usually a confession of what is already in your heart. Out of your heart flows the issues and concerns that are spoken through your mouth.

If you think and meditate long and hard enough about a situation, it will eventually flow from your thoughts and from your mouth.

There is amazing power in the tongue and in the spoken word, but you can fight and overcome this deadly trap by:

- Speaking the truth of the Word of God in love.
- Always saying what God says about you.
- Understanding when to speak, when to pray, and when to be quiet.
- Understanding that your words are powerful and can create either a great destiny for you or they can bring devastation to your life.
- Studying to be quiet and slow to speak.
- Not rehearsing in your mind or speaking out everything you hear, see, or believe.
- Using your mouth and your words to lift up, build up, and edify others.

What negative things have I been saying about myself? How can I change this?

_____
_____
_____
_____
_____
_____
_____
_____
_____
_____
_____
_____
_____
_____
_____
_____
_____
_____

Personal Notes/Reflection

Sin Trap
Chapter 9

For all have sinned and fall short of the glory of God. Romans 3:23 (NIV)

For the wages of sin is death, but the gift of God is eternal life in Christ Jesus our Lord. Romans 6:23 (NIV)

Therefore confess your sins to each other and pray for each other so that you may be healed. The prayer of a righteous man is powerful and effective. James 5:16 (NIV)

Sin! All of us have sinned and fallen short of God's standard. There is no one who can say they have not sinned, except Christ Jesus. The Bible says, "*We were born in sin and shaped in iniquity*" (Psalm 51:5). Sin knocks on every door, and it is a decision of your will whether you open the door and invite it in. Sin cannot enter your life without an invitation from you.

Let me illustrate. Sin comes knocking at your door and you go to the door and ask who is there, and the reply is sin. You then decide to have a conversation with it by asking what it wants. It replies, "Won't you open the door and let me in so we can discuss it?" You say, 'Just a minute please.' The moment you hesitate, it gains an entrance because it knows it is enticing you. You then open the door and invite it in. It comes in with such force that it will devastate your life and will be very difficult to dislodge and send it packing. Doesn't that sound like a foolish analogy? Unfortunately, many times this is what we do. We open the door and allow sin to come in because it seems harmless, and we think we can handle it. The sin trap of the enemy is to ensure that you are never free to love God completely, love yourself fully, or to love others as God decrees. Sin keeps you blinded to your own faults while pointing out the faults of others. Sin evicted Adam and Eve out of the Garden of Eden. They were enticed away from a paradise that God had so lovingly prepared for them. One day, sin came knocking; and they invited it in never fully realizing the devastation it would cause not only to their lives but also to the whole human race. Since that day, sin has run rampant in our lives. Sin arrives in many shapes and forms.

You sin against God when you disobey His commands and instructions. You also sin when you reject His ways and His plans for your life by choosing to do things your way and in your own strength. You sin against yourself and against others when you neglect to confess your wrongdoings. You also sin against people when you have scorn, bitterness and unforgiveness towards them. Let us look at an example of what sin did to Adam and Eve's first two children.

What sins have kept me in the enemy's trap?

_____

_____

_____

_____

_____

_____

Adam lay with his wife Eve, and she became pregnant and gave birth to Cain. She said, "With the help of the Lord I have brought forth a man." Later she gave birth to his brother Abel. Now Abel kept flocks, and Cain worked the soil. In the course of time Cain brought some of the fruits of the soil as an offering to the Lord. But Able brought fat portions from some of the firstborn of his flock. The Lord looked with favor on Abel and his offering, but on Cain and his offering he did not look with favor. So, Cain was very angry, and his face was downcast. Then the Lord said to Cain, "Why are you angry? Why is your face downcast? If you do what is right, will you not be accepted? But if you do not do what is right, sin is crouching at your door; it desires to have you, but you must master it." Now Cain said to his brother Abel, "Let's go out to the field." And while they were in the field, Cain attacked his brother Abel and killed him. Then the Lord said to Cain, "Where is your brother Abel?" "I don't know," he re plied. "Am I my brother's keeper?" Genesis 4:19 (NIV)

Adam and Eve were driven out of the Garden of Eden, and they began reproducing as God had stipulated. Their firstborn was a son. They named him Cain and were very proud of him. His name meant, "To acquire." I imagine when they gave birth to Cain, they probably thought their punishment was not as bad as they expected when God expelled them from the garden and secured it so they could not reenter because they had great joy at his birth. They gave birth to another child whom they named Abel. His name meant, "Breath or vapor." How extremely accurate were their names. Their names truly signified what their characters would be. Cain would try to get possession of what was not his.

He would seek to acquire the blessings and favor God had given to Abel because Abel gave his best offering to God. Abel's life was only temporary because Cain killed him prematurely. After this incident, Adam and Eve began to experience the painful results of sin. They experienced the pain of grief. In their grief, they probably gained a good understanding of how Jehovah God must have felt when they sinned, and their sin separated them from Him. They began to experience the pain of their own disobedience because of their sins. Their pain must have been devastating, a pain they never expected or experienced before. I am sure their grief was unbearable, and they caught a glimpse of how God must have felt when He found they had disobeyed His instructions, and He had to distance Himself from His children.

The sin of jealousy and competition produced the first murder ever recorded in the Bible. It is evident Cain had plotted and meditated on what he would do to his brother, and he waited for an opportunity to carry out his plan. He approached his brother Abel and invited him out to the field. This was probably a very natural occurrence for them so there was no reason for Abel to be suspicious. Abel went with his brother not knowing sin had caused Cain's heart to be bitter and unforgiving toward him. Cain's sin caused him to kill Abel without hesitation. When God questioned him, he lied without hesitation. He told God he did not know where his brother was, and he appeared to have an attitude. He answered God by asking if he was his brother's keeper. There was no repentance in Cain's heart for what he had done. He was caught in the sin trap and did not yet understand there was a way out. 1 John 1:9 (NIV) says, *"If we confess our sins, he is faithful and just and will forgive us our sins and purify us from all unrighteousness."* Cain had a way of escape. He could have asked for God's pardon and forgiveness, but he chose not to.

You can get off this cycle quickly and effectively by following these easy steps:
- Be honest with yourself and admit that you are in sin.
- Confess your sins to God.
- Declare, say out loud, exclaim to God what you have done and are doing.
- Find a trustworthy friend and confess your fault and sin to them.
- Repent and turn away from the sin by going down a different path.
- Understand you have the power of the Holy Spirit to help you be victorious.
- Choose to walk out of darkness and into God's marvelous light.
- Choose God's plan for your life instead of your own plans.
- Romans 5:20 says *where sin abounds, grace does much more abound.*
- Know that grace flows in abundance to your life when sin tries to overrun it.
- Remember grace grows out of measure and runs over its brink to flood your life in the midst of your sin.
- See God's grace as a stream which is always flowing freely toward you.
- Remember the flood of sin cannot surpass the flood of grace God has made available to you.

Poverty Mentality Trap
Chapter 10

Beloved, I wish above all things that thou mayest prosper and be in health, even as thy soul prospereth. John 1:2 (KJV)

The devil has convinced believers, and nonbelievers alike, that to be poor is okay and that it is even spiritual. He has you believing the lie that there is nothing wrong with living from paycheck to paycheck. He wants you to believe God will only supply your basic needs and no more. He has told you God is not in the business of giving you more, nor does He want you to live in abundance. Philippians 4:19 disputes that lie. God has promised to supply all your needs according to His riches in glory by Christ Jesus. It is His intention to shower you with riches for your daily life.

On a recent mission trip to San Pedro Sula, Honduras, I saw the devastating trap of poverty. My team and I went to a village we named the Riverside Community to assess the needs and to see if we could provide aid to the people living there. I was reminded the poverty mentality trap so many of us have been caught in has much to do with our environment. In the Riverside community we noticed there were no water wells. We saw the people drinking the same water they bathed in. Poverty was all around them and a trap had been set up in their environment to enslave them. Many of them were falling into it because in their minds they had no other options, and seemingly no way out.

3 John 1:2 gives you a clear picture of God's heart and desires toward you. He wishes, He desires, He yearns and hopes above all else that you prosper. To prosper means to be successful in your endeavors. Not only does He want your material needs to be met, but He also wants you to be in health even as you experience soul prosperity in your emotions, relationships, spirit, and in your finances. He desires for your soul to be satisfied in Him and with His provisions for your life. He wants you to experience peace and to be at rest.

While resting, you will experience oneness with Him. He wants healthy families and healthy relationships. He intends our marriages to be a place of personal growth, blessings, sharing, protection, and character development. His intention is for you to have sound relationships with your earthly brothers and sisters as well as the spiritual ones. God designed you to have unity and oneness which is where He commands the blessings in your life. When your soul is prospering, you have soundness of mind and emotions and are not easily tossed around by every wind of doctrine or the beliefs of others. You will have your own set of beliefs and develop your own strong belief system.

As you prosper and come into health, you will be free to love God completely, to experience His amazing fullness in your life, and to find His very best for you in every situation. God de sires that you come to know Him as a Father, Friend, Protector, Helper, and the One who will stand with you and for you no matter what you face. He sent Jesus so you will not be poor in spirit or in mind so you could live life on earth as you will live it out in heaven, completely fulfilled, satisfied, trusting, and depending on His mercies. He wants you to overflow with everlasting joy in your life. Poverty mentality is a deadly trap because it will keep you from expecting much out of life and stop you from striving for more from God. God did not design you to be poor in spirit, poor in mind, poor in health, poor financially or poor in any area of your life. He is a God of abundance.

I understand the Word says we will always have the poor with us, but you don't have to be one of the poor! You were not designed to live in lack in any area of your life. God designed you with the mindset of living in abundance. He wants you to have an abundance of health and wealth that will overflow from your life to the lives of others who are in need of your assistance. God designed you to be free from a poverty mentality and to experience prosperity in Him in all facets of life.

You can overcome poverty mentality by replacing those thoughts with thoughts of:

- Blessings.
- Prosperity.
- Health.
- Wealth.
- Abundance in life.
- Favor in all situations.
- And understanding God wants you to prosper and be in perfect health even as you experience prosperity in your soul.

How have I been caught in the poverty mentality trap?

_____

_____

_____

_____

_____

_____

_____

_____

_____

Personal Notes/Reflection

Approval Trap
Chapter 11

Owe no man anything, but to love one another: for he that loveth another hath fulfilled the law.

Romans 13:8 (KJV)

While attending high school I had an incident that has never left my memory. I am reminded of so many young adults who are feeling the pressure to be approved and accepted. There was a very bossy group of young ladies who were part of the "in crowd," or so it seemed in high school. They made it their duty to ask very personal questions of those they thought needed their attention and approval. I watched them many times making the rounds of students whom they thought were intimidated by them, and who did not hesitate to answer and agree with their assessment about those students' lives. These students were seeking approval; and, if they received it from the people who were considered popular, they believed they would gain acceptance.

One day, one of the bolder students in the group decided to approach me and began asking personal questions. I simply stared at her as she began her interrogation and did not respond. She asked me if I was going to answer her questions and I told her the answers were none of her business. I suggested she move on to someone else who was more susceptible to her questioning and who needed her attention. I did not need or want her attention and was not looking for approval from her or any of her friends. I must tell you; she was completely taken back and expressed her surprise at my response. She walked away and related my response to her buddies. They learned by this encounter that there were a few students who did not need or want their approval to be who they were created to be.

We have all been pulled into the approval trap at one time or another because we desire to be accepted by the people who are around us. Approval means to accept as is, to like, support, recognize, and to endorse. You are pulled into this trap because of a desire to be a part of a group, a team, or even a family environment. Other times you are pulled into this trap because you desire to hear that you have done something good.

I have taught the Word of God for a long time, and over the years I found myself wanting people to tell me the messages were good and helpful to their lives. Often people would share with me that the messages indeed blessed them, but there were also times when there was no feedback. The times when no one approached or encouraged me were times I had to work hard to keep from being discouraged and wondering if I had been effective in what I taught. I was seeking approval from those who heard the messages.

It has been a long journey getting to the place where I accept that all God asks of me is to do my best and to be pleasing to Him. Over the last several years, after each message, I ask God these questions. Did I do what You instructed me to? Did I allow You to flow through me to impact lives? Were You pleased with the message that was shared? I discovered His answers and His endorsement meant more than a thousand people telling me they were blessed. The lesson for was to be more concerned about pleasing God than pleasing people. Our desire to please people is why we are caught in the approval trap. I have continued to work on ensuring God is pleased with my efforts.

Sometimes the desire to be approved by others can cause you to get involved in the wrong relationships, making bad choices and decisions, or settling for less than you deserve. Many times, you do not receive all God has planned for you because you are looking for and expecting less than His best for you. The encounter I had with those students while in school has happened many times since. It has happened on the job, at churches, and in smaller groups.

I will be the first to admit it is easier to go along with the crowd than to make a stand for what is right and best for you. It can be lonely when you take the stand not to be trapped in the cycle of needing someone's approval to be who you are. I have been able to stand firm in several instances because of the foundation I received while growing up, as well as the lessons learned when I have sought to please others. I have also learned many lessons from observing close friends and relatives who made wrong decisions because they felt the pressure of the crowd.

When you choose not to get caught in the approval trap, you might experience some loneliness for a time, but God always rewards you for taking a stand for what is right. You can never choose to do right and not be victorious in the end. Since approval means you accept others as is, you must decide what situation will work best for your life. Here is an example. Many of you will make a choice concerning the person you choose as a life-mate. Often there is more than one option available to you, but you choose the person you feel is most compatible. You choose the qualities or quirks you can live with. In addition, you also choose the person with the temperament you feel you can live with daily. Remember, you will always have a choice to make in every life changing situation.

The desire to be approved by people can be detrimental to your decision. Here is why! No man or woman can approve you. They do not have the ability to approve who you are or who you will become. Most of them have their own issues and will often filter your situation through theirs. They will give you advice based on what they would do; not necessarily what is most suited or beneficial to you. You cannot find the answers for your life by someone else's opinions or recommendations. You cannot find it in the things you have attained to be accepted and welcomed into the in-crowd. God is the only one who can give you His stamp of approval. He created you and knew everything about you. He formed you in secret and made deposits of greatness in you that no one else can bring out of you but Him.

He has stamped you as unique and special which means He has already approved you.

I have learned since He has given you His stamp of approval, you don't need it from others to succeed. You will realize after a while, that those who would attempt to change you into their image will eventually get on board when God begins to manifest His glory through you. The approval of others is not necessary for you to live a full life. They do not have the right to sanction what God has spoken to your heart about your life. They are not qualified to tell you how to live and what to do. They have difficulty living their own lives. Others can encourage and support you but cannot approve what God has assigned for you. There is only One with that authority, and His name is Father God.

The above scripture encourages you to owe no man anything but to love one another. Love does not give others the right to run your life or to tell you how to live. Love means you are accepted as you are and welcomed into the family or group. If you owe someone anything other than love, they will expect payment. Some people may think a good form of payment is to fall into their plans and do what they say instead of what you know is right for you. Often you are caught in this approval trap because you feel indebted to someone. They have been there for you and helped in many situations, so you feel you owe it to them. As a result, you bend over backwards to please them. Some of those people will be demanding, and you must draw a line in the sand and decide whether you owe them.

Love means you stand up for yourself and for what you believe. It does not require you to turn your life completely over to someone else's control. God is the only One who can rightly approve you. As you seek to please Him, He will ensure others come in alignment. Trust Him only, as you reach for approval in your life; and do not let this trap of the enemy keep you from experiencing the fullness of God in all areas of your life.

To overcome this trap, remember:
- How greatly loved you are.
- God has already placed His stamp of approval on you.
- You have the right to think your own thoughts and live your own life.
- God has a specific purpose for your life.
- God is the only one who knows all there is to know about you, you only need His approval to succeed.
- You do not owe anyone for your existence so do not turn control over to anyone but God.

What things have caused me to be caught in the approval trap?

_____

_____

_____

_____

_____

_____

_____

Prayer for Overcoming the Traps

Father, I thank You for revealing to me the many traps of the enemy. I know there are other traps You will reveal to me in my walk with You. Today, I ask Your help to overcome the specific trap in my life that I have encountered which has caused me to be ineffective in the things You have asked me to do. I ask You to help me to overcome the self-sufficiency trap, and to realize how much I need Your help and guidance. Where I have been disobedient and unwilling to do things Your way, I ask Your forgiveness.

Forgive me for the things I have thought about and meditated on that did not glorify You. These things have not been profitable for my life. I take control of my thought life, in Jesus' name. Help me to put a guard over my mouth. I will watch what I speak over myself and over others, in Jesus' name. Jesus, the sin trap has kept me living below what You died on Calvary to give me, so I ask Your help to overcome it, in Jesus' name.

I confess my sins to You and ask You to help me live for You each day. I need the Holy Spirit's help to live a life that is pleasing to You. Help me not to do anything that will bring shame to Your name. The poverty mentality trap was designed to keep me from Your best in life, and I ask You to help me to renew my mind daily with Your Word. You desire me to prosper and be in perfect health even as my soul prospers, and I thank You that You have given Your all so I will be blessed.

Jesus, help me to know the only approval I need comes from You, the Father, and the Holy Spirit. You have already approved me by going to the cross of Calvary. I thank You that I have the power of the Holy Spirit living in me, and I know with Him I am more than a conqueror through Jesus Christ. Thanks for helping me overcome these traps, and for causing me to be aware when the enemy tries to trap me in other situations of my life. I ask Your blessing over my life and the lives of my loved ones, in Jesus' name. Amen!

Personal Notes/Reflection

The Believer's Protection

Your Authority in the Battle
Chapter 12

I have given you authority to trample on snakes and scorpions and to overcome all the power of the enemy; nothing will harm you. Luke 10:19 (NIV)

You have been given power and authority over all the power of the enemy. Therefore, you can command the devil to flee from you in the name of Jesus and he must flee. He has no right or authority to come into your presence and to traumatize you. God has given you His authority because of the price Jesus paid on Calvary. He has given you power, rights, title, prestige, rule, control, and dominion over the devil and his tactics. We originally lost our authority when Adam and Eve gave their power away in the Garden of Eden. God created them to rule and to reign, but they were enticed by the enemy and gave away their right to dominate, rule and govern the earth.

The above scripture gives a clear picture of what believers look like when they walk in the authority that has been given to them. Jesus said He has given you authority to trample on snakes yet, when you and I hear the word snake, we have an instant reaction, one of fear, revulsion, and intimidation; and we get a picture of a deadly creature. The mere thought of encountering such a creature gives us the shakes. We know if a snake bites us, the con sequences could be deadly. It is interesting to note Jesus has given you power and authority over the very thing that tempted and stole Adam and Eve's power and authority in the gar den. He said you can trample – crush, grind, squash, and stamp out the enemy.

Those are strong words, giving you a clear picture of your authority and the power behind it. You can crush the life out of the enemy's attempt to ruin and gain authority over you. You can nullify, stop, and overcome every ploy of the enemy. When you overcome something or someone, you vanquish them from your presence; and you have the power to subdue their effect in your life. Jesus says you can overcome the devil's power and blot out his presence from your life, and He goes on to say that you have the same power over scorpions.

The power in the scorpion's tail destroys him after he has made one venomous sting. Jesus used two of the deadliest creatures to give you a vivid picture of how His power and authority in your life can make the enemy's deadly poison null and void. He explicitly states you can trample on them, and they will not harm you.

In Acts chapter twenty-eight, the Apostle Paul had an encounter with a snake when he was shipwrecked on the shore of Malta. Because of his faith and conviction about the Lord Jesus Christ, He was sailing to Rome as a prisoner to stand trial. The ship encountered a storm. The storm was fierce, and the people feared for their lives. The Lord gave Paul a message to share with the passengers. He said, "I urge you to keep up your courage because not one of you will be lost; only the ship will be destroyed." Imagine the destruction of a ship without one life lost. God honored His word to Paul, not one life was lost, and they ended up on the Island of Malta. Once they were safely ashore, the islanders showed them unusual kindness. As they built a fire to welcome them, Paul gathered a pile of wood; and, as he was putting the wood on the fire, a snake, driven out by the heat of the fire, latched onto Paul's hand. Paul shook the snake into the fire. The islanders were observing him said one to the other, "This man must be a murderer, for though he es caped from the sea, justice has not allowed him to live." Naturally, they expected him to die. The islanders expected Paul to swell up and die suddenly because this had been their experience in the past; but after a long while Paul remained alive. They thought he was a god. They had never witnessed the survival of anyone bitten by that snake who survived without any medical attention. It is apparent Paul understood the scripture which said no deadly thing shall by any means harm him.

Am I saying for you to go and pick up these deadly creatures or to trample on them? No! What I am saying is there is a promise in God's Word for every believer. If you do encounter them, and you know God is your source of help, He will give you the power to shake off their deadly power over your life. This holds true both in the natural and spiritual realm. When you come under attack by the devil, you have the power to shake him off and crush him by re minding him who you are, in the name of Jesus. Remember, Jesus gives this power to you. You are not able to withstand the enemy in your own power and authority. You need the help of the Holy Spirit to overcome him every time to be victorious.

What is my authority in God and how do I use it?

_____

_____

_____

_____

_____

_____

_____

_____

_____

_____

Boldness

They had Peter and John brought before them and began to question them: "By what power or what name did you do this?" Then Peter, filled with the Holy Spirit, said to them: "Rulers and elders of the people! If we are being called to account today for an act of kindness shown to a cripple and are asked how he was healed, then know this, you and all the people of Israel: It is by the name of Jesus Christ of Nazareth, whom you crucified but whom God raised from the dead, that this man stands before you healed. He is the stone you builders rejected, which has become the capstone. Salvation is found in no one else, for there is no other name under heaven given to men by which we must be saved." Acts 4:712 (NIV)

With your authority, you have been given boldness that will enable you to stand in the face of adverse situations. This boldness comes when you come face-to-face with the risen Christ and accept His gift of the Holy Spirit's power to work in your life. Without His power working in and through you, you will be helpless, powerless, and easily defeated.

When you encounter the risen Christ in the way the Apostle Peter did, after failing many tests in his walk with the Lord, God will also give you boldness to walk in the authority He has given to you. Peter walked in boldness and authority after he was filled with the power of the Holy Spirit. The scripture says he healed a man who had been crippled from birth; and, as a result, he came under attack by the Jews. In boldness, he told the people that apart from Christ, they were helpless, hopeless, and lost. He also told them that he was not ashamed of the Gospel of Christ because he fully understood that salvation could not be found in any other person but the person of Jesus Christ. Prior to his encounter with the Holy Spirit, Peter was fearful; not effective in his Christian walk, and his faith was weak. When he encountered the Holy Spirit on the day of Pentecost (Acts 2), his life was radically changed, and he was filled with boldness. The Holy Spirit's power enabled him to use his God-given authority and to be bold as a lion for the cause of Christ.

When he and the others were threatened by the Jews and told not to speak in the name of Jesus, they refused to obey. Can you imagine being told not to speak that precious name? What would you do in this situation? Would you speak or would you remain silent? They had a choice to make; and they decided that regardless of the trials or the outcome, they would indeed speak the precious name of Jesus. It was impossible for them not to speak about what they had seen and heard. Peter's boldness was astonishing because just a few weeks earlier, in the same place, before the same people, because of fear, he had denied Jesus three times. Once he experienced the love, forgiveness, and the power of the Holy Spirit, he boldly and fearlessly defended and stood up for the same Jesus whom he had previously denied.

Peter discovered fire and power within himself when the believers, in unity, stood up to the Jews and continued to declare the name of Jesus. When you are unified in your beliefs and your faith, boldness is released in your heart. Unity means oneness, and to be joined with others to create greater wholeness. It signifies harmony and agreement and means to be in one accord in your attitudes, opinions, and intentions. The apostles and the believers were unified with a demonstration of boldness and power because of their unity. After that encounter, they discovered when they were unified, they were powerful. Your unity will bring about the power that you need to showcase to the world who God is in your life.

When you know your rightful place and the authority you have been given by Jesus, you will take a stand and believe for change. You have been given authority in the battles you face. You have the backing of the Godhead when you stand for what is right and good. Each time the Lord gives you directions about standing firm in your authority, you must know He will always be there to ensure you are victorious. You have authority to speak to every mountain in your life and know that it must move out of your way. Stand on the many promises in the Word of God and be dressed in your armor to win every fight. The Apostles Paul and Peter faced many difficult circumstances, but they understood their authority and walked in it. They trusted that God would back them every step of the way, and He did. Jesus died to redeem our authority that was stolen from Adam and Eve by the devil. After He redeemed our authority, He gave it back to every believer. The enemy no longer has the power to control your thoughts, decisions, or you. Stand firm in the authority and boldness has been returned to you. Know you have the authority to annihilate the enemy in every battle you face. You have authority to trample, crush, grind, squash, vanquish, and stamp out the enemy not only in your life, but also in the lives of your loved ones, in Jesus' name. I encourage you to pray and never stop praying, then stand and see the salvation of the Lord unfold in the midst of the battle.

How bold am I in my faith and for the cause of Christ? Explain.

_____

_____

_____

_____

_____

_____

_____

_____

_____

_____

Prayer of Authority

Father, in the name of Jesus, I thank You for giving me the authority to stand strong in the battles I face. I thank You because Jesus went to the cross of Calvary, and took back the authority given to the devil, I am now victorious. Help me to take up my authority and walk in boldness in every situation I face. Remind me daily, You have given me the power to overcome the devil's attempts to convince me that I have no power and authority over him.

Jesus, I understand You have all authority in Your hands, and You have transferred it to me. Give me the courage to take up my authority and not to shrink back from the attacks of the enemy, but to face him head-on knowing that I am backed by the Godhead (Father, Son, and Holy Spirit). I understand I cannot fight and win on my own, so I trust You to give me wisdom, guide my every step, and every decision, in Jesus' name.

Give me Your amazing peace in the midst of the storm and allow me to walk in Your authority. I trust Your guidance and leadership, and I come to You in boldness and confidence knowing You said if I asked it will be given to me. I am asking in Jesus' name that You remove the spirit of timidity from me and fill me with power and boldness to accomplish everything You have planned for my life. Thank You for helping me to overcome by the blood of the Lamb and the word of my testimony. My testimony is I can do all things through Christ who strengthens me, in Jesus' name.

Amen!

Personal Notes/Reflection

Belt of Truth
Chapter 13

Finally, be strong in the Lord and in His mighty power. Put on the full armor of God so that you can take your stand against the devil's schemes. For our struggle is not against flesh and blood, but against the rulers, against the authorities, against the powers of this dark world and against the spiritual forces of evil in the heavenly realms. Therefore, put on the full armor of God, so that when the day of evil comes, you may be able to stand your ground, and after you have done everything, to stand. Stand firm then, with the belt of truth buckled around your waist, with the breastplate of righteousness in place, and with your feet fitted with the readiness that comes from the gospel of peace. In addition to all this, take up the shield of faith, with which you can extinguish all the flaming arrows of the evil one. Take the helmet of salvation and the sword of the Spirit, which is the word of God. And pray in the Spirit on all occasions with all kinds of prayers and requests. With this in mind, be alert and always keep on praying for all the saints. Ephesians 6:1018 (NIV)

As we explore the protection God has given to every believer by providing us with the armor of God, I want you to know there are thousands of promises in the Word of God for you. Ephesians 6 begins our discovery of the protective armor that is available to you with a strong command from the Lord, *"Finally, be strong in the Lord and His mighty power."* When I read this scripture, I get a picture of God telling us to do something we already have the power to do. He is not saying, "I hope you are strong in the Lord, or, please be strong in the Lord, but "Be strong!" It is a command that makes it clear you have the power and ability within you to be strong in whatever battle you face. The command to be strong is necessary when you understand you have supernatural enemies, and you are in a fight with the devil who is determined to win.

Since you have supernatural enemies, you need both supernatural power and the armor of God to defeat them in your life. You have a supernatural armor you must put on every day to be successful. This armor consists of seven pieces. Seven is the number of completion, so your success is guaranteed. When you dress yourself daily in this armor, you can withstand the devil's schemes, tactics, deception, and his cunning ways. A significant part of your armor is to declare what God says about you in the Word. You must consistently and actively speak the Word of God over your life. The scriptures tell us to stand against the devil's schemes, stand against the day of evil, stand with the belt of truth around our waist, and to keep standing after we have done everything. Never give up! You will overcome the work of the enemy by standing firm on the Word of God. You must stay battle-ready for whenever and however the enemy will try to attack you. 1 Peter 5:8 (KJV) gives a clear picture of what staying battle ready looks like. It encourages you to *"Be sober, be vigilant; because your adversary the devil, as a roaring lion, walketh about, seeking whom he may devour."* The enemy is on the prowl looking for people, who are "sleeping on the job."

They are unaware a battle is raging; they need to be alert and aware of what they are facing.

Though the enemy is on the prowl, he is not greater than the power of God that lives in you. The power that lives in you is the same power that raised Jesus from the dead. As a result of this amazing power, you can stand against the storm and face the roaring lion with confidence you have already been given victory over him.

The armor of God has both defensive as well as offensive pieces, to guarantee your success. Ephesians 6:14 introduces the most important piece of the armor, "the belt of truth." The Roman Soldier's belt held many of the other pieces of the seven-piece armor together because most of the pieces hang from the belt. In modern day clothing, a belt is often necessary for people to be properly clothed, and so is the belt of truth. The belt of truth is the written Word of God and is a most effective piece of weaponry. The Bible says the Word of God is truth.

During the first century, a soldier's ability to use his weapons depended heavily on his belt. Without the belt, the soldier would not be properly equipped for battle. The belt of truth is the Word of God and is essential to every believer. God's truth is absolute and not subjective. You cannot pick and choose which scriptures to believe and apply then ignore the rest of it. God's Word is the whole counsel of God. It must be accepted, believed, and applied as such. As the Word becomes central to your life, it will always keep you focused on Jesus, the only true source of help in your battle. God's Word gives clear insight to what He has provided for you, it keeps your thoughts aligned with His will. It protects your mind like a powerful helmet and keeps you focused on the truth in all situations.

The belt of truth, the Word of God, is the piece of the armor no believer can success fully live without. Psalm 119:105 tells us the Word is a lamp unto our feet and a light to our path. This means the Word gives direction as well as illumination, so your feet will locate the right path to your destination. The Word gives you assurance and reassurance as you begin faithfully walking in the direction leading you to victory. The Word is powerful, central, and necessary for your survival in this day and time. When you understand the Word of God is your lifeline, your vitality, your spark, and your life force, you will see how essential it is for your existence. It makes you steady, firm, and secure in battle because it is the only foundation for life.

How does God's Word work in my life?

_____

_____

_____

_____

Personal Notes/Reflection

Breastplate of Righteousness
Chapter 14

With the breastplate of righteousness in place. Ephesians 6:14b (NIV)

When something covers the breast area, it protects your heart. God has given you a breastplate of righteousness to protect the most vital organ in your body, your heart. This breastplate of righteousness means the condition acceptable by God for every believer. It is the exchange of our sins for His righteousness. You cannot do anything to earn or nullify its power in your life. Righteousness means you have right standing with God. It speaks of godliness, morality, being upright, and having virtue. These qualities can only be realized because of Jesus' sacrifice for us; not in our own strength or power. It took the sinless, spotless Lamb of God to achieve this righteous ness for you and me. Your obedience to Him signifies your heart agrees with God, and it displays the genuineness of your faith in Him. As you choose to obey God, you demonstrate your love for Him, and a will do what is pleasing and acceptable to Him.

It takes faith in God to become all He has destined for you, and your faith connects the breastplate of righteousness with God's infinite power to begin operating in you. The breast plate of righteousness covers your heart. Because of the washing and cleansing power of the blood of Jesus, the devil will not be able to find one single thing to exploit in your life.

Loving others helps you keep the breastplate of righteousness in place. When you love, you demonstrate you are walking and living in the love of God that has been deposited into your heart. It also shows that you understand who you are in Him. The display of His righteous ness and amazing love brings forgiveness. It cleanses you no matter what you have done. When you receive that love and pass it on to others, the world will see a true example of the nature of God.

Love will show people that forgiveness and grace is extended to them, and they simply must reach out and receive it. Because of God's love for you, the Apostle Paul writes in Romans 8 there is no condemnation for those who are in Christ Jesus. Through Christ Jesus the law of the Spirit of life has set you free from the law of sin and death. This is a clear promise from the Lord because you are His righteousness God says He does not condemn you. Condemnation fills you with a feeling of unworthiness, guilt, shame, blame, and a feeling of being judged. It is clear from these definitions condemnation does not come from God but from the enemy. He is the one who makes you feel unworthy and fills you with guilt and shame. He brings condemnation so you will not ask for forgiveness or seek help from the Lord.

I have counseled many people over the years, and the greatest struggle many fight is this feeling of condemnation due to sin and bad choices. They feel unworthy, believe they will never be forgiven, and no one will forget what they have done. These feelings keep them in a cycle of defeat with a sense they have nothing to contribute to society. All of you have value and have much to contribute to your family, friends, job, and the world.

How does the Holy Spirit correct you when you sin and miss the mark? His correction comes in the form of conviction. He gently reminds you that you are off course and in error; and He gives you an opportunity to repent, turn away from it, and to return to Him. His conviction does not make you feel unworthy or valueless. Conviction brings correction to your heart and enables you to examine what is in your heart so you will do what is right and pleasing to the Lord.

The breastplate of righteousness protects your heart. It guards your mind, soul, and emotions from the devil's accusations which are designed to bring guilt and shame to you. Proverbs 11 says the righteousness of the upright delivers them, but the unfaithful are trapped by evil desires. Righteousness will bring you deliverance and will always bring you to a place of safe ty and victory. You are the righteousness of God in Christ Jesus (2 Cor. 5:21) the sacrifice Jesus made gives you freedom from your past, present, and future sins. Once and for all, His blood sets you free from the penalty of sin. The Bible says in 1 John 1:9 (NIV) – "*If we confess our sins, He is faithful and just and will forgive us our sins and purify us from all unrighteousness.*" You have access to God to receive pardon, forgiveness, and cleansing from all past failures and sins. God knew mankind would sin and miss the mark, so He provided a way for us to live our days free from condemnation and guilt. The breastplate of righteousness keeps you from being overtaken

How has the righteousness of God kept me from the enemy's attacks on my mind?

_____
_____
_____
_____
_____
_____
_____
_____
_____

Shield of Faith
Chapter 15

In addition to all this, take up the shield of faith, with which you can extinguish all the flaming arrows of the evil one. Ephesians 6:16 (NIV)

A shield speaks to me of safety, covering, protection, and refuge. In battle, a shield keeps the weapons of destruction away from your heart, and it preserves your life. The Roman soldier's shield was such a covering. It resembled our modern-day doors which provide protection for the people inside the building. It was wide and long enough to completely cover the soldier's body. The Apostle Paul compares your faith to the Roman soldier's shield. God is saying He has provided you with enough faith to completely cover you in every situation and every battle. God has given you the measure of faith (Romans 12:3), enough faith to be sure you are successful and will not be destroyed in the battles of life.

The soldier's shield was covered with six layers of animal hide which were tightly woven together, it was extremely durable, and fit for battle. Each day the soldiers would rub oil into the leather to soften it because it was necessary to keep the leather soft and supple to deflect the enemy's weapons. The soldiers understood the daily routine of oiling the leather was absolutely necessary so it would not become stiff, hard and crack. If their shield broke apart during battle, their lives were at stake. Your faith requires the same degree of anointing, so you do not easily crack or break in the battles of life.

Time spent with the Holy Spirit each day increases your faith to receive fresh revelations about what to do and how to be an overcomer in all situations. Your faith will go through much testing, and it will stand strong, if you remember you need help to sustain yourself, and be victorious. The shield of faith keeps the darts of the devil from penetrating your heart and mind, and from causing severe damage to your life. Your faith may not hold up in the battle if you do not immerse yourself daily in the presence and power of the Holy Spirit. Seek the anointing to keep your faith fresh and alive because it is your shield of protection, and faith quenches the fiery darts of the enemy.

Romans chapter ten says faith comes by hearing the message, and the message is heard through the Word of God. Your faith is developed and will thrive when you hear messages that are rooted in the Word. The Words of God are words of faith, and they are designed to transform and change your life. The written Word has the power to change your situation when you receive and apply it to your life. As you read and study the Word, God will give you the exact word that is needed for your situation. Let us look at an example.

When they came to the crowd, a man approached Jesus and knelt before him. "Lord, have mercy on my son," he said. "He has seizures and is suffering greatly. He often falls into the fire or into the water. I brought him to your disciples, but they could not heal him." "O unbelieving and perverse generation," Jesus replied, "how long shall I stay with you? How long shall I put up with you? Bring the boy here to me." Jesus rebuked the demon, and it came out of the boy, and he was healed from that moment. Then the disciples came to Jesus in private and asked, "Why couldn't we drive it out?" He replied, "Because you have so little faith I tell you the truth, if you have faith as small as a mustard seed, you can say to this mountain, 'Move from here to there' and it will move. Nothing will be impossible for you"

(Matthew 17:1420 (NIV).

Faith is required for moving the mountains of sickness, debt, fear, and lack from your life. The above scripture verses give a clear indication of the disciples' hearts. They wanted to see the young boy healed, and they tried, but they were unsuccessful. The boy's desperate father, went to the Source, Jesus, to get the right kind of help. He told Jesus he had gone to the disciples for help, but they were unable to help him. I do not believe he was pointing his finger at the disciples' lack of ability, he simply wanted Jesus to know that before coming to Him, he had sought help from others. He learned through his experience help could only be found in Jesus, the true Source of life. Jesus spoke specific words to the tormenting spirits and commanded them to release the boy. They had no option but to obey His voice and set the boy free.

Several years ago, I was ministering a message on mustard seed faith. I went on a hunt to find mustard seeds because I wanted to see how small these seeds were. When I found them, I was amazed to discover the seeds were so small several of them could comfortably fit under my thumbnail. The day before delivering the message, I sat down and placed one small seed into a few hundred envelopes. The next morning, I went to the class and handed out the envelopes with instructions to the attendees not to open them. The class was very curious about what was in the envelope. Many people thought I had given them a sealed envelope with nothing in it. As the class ended, I spoke to them about having faith as the grain of a mustard seed, and then told them to open the envelope and look at the actual size of the mustard seed. Many were amazed that Jesus was telling them, if they had faith as small as that seed, they could move mountains in their lives. I further explained that Jesus said, "If you have faith as small as a grain of a mustard seed." He was saying that within the small mustard seed there were grains, which were even smaller than the actual seed itself, and they did not need much faith to be victorious. Jesus is also telling you only a small grain of faith is required to move the mountains in your life. This demonstration was time consuming but effective.

The shield of faith is your guarantee of success when you face the mountains. It is a powerful weapon to use, as you begin to live out the call of God on your life, and to fight the battles you face. Faith believes, despite the natural facts, circumstances, or what people say; and it perseveres by helping you push through life's difficulties and adversities. Faith will take you to the battle and keep you there when it gets difficult. Your faith grows through the trials you endure and overcome. It is developed and strengthened through difficult situations and circumstances, and it matures you, when you realize you are not in control and learn to turn all things over to God.

When you take up the shield of faith, you will find the courage and determination to win and always expect the right outcome. The shield protects you in the battles because you are fortified, as you march forward, refusing to allow the devil to intimidate you. Here are the rewards for your faith:

- You will receive the full manifestation for what you believe.
- As you ask, it will be given to you.
- As you seek, you will find.
- You will accomplish all God has called you to do when you choose faith over fear.
- You will be abundantly prosperous because faith rewards.
- You will live a life of joy, peace, and victory because faith always wins.
- You will enjoy every moment of your life, and no days will ever be wasted.
- True faith in God will cause you to succeed in everything you put your hands to.

I charge you to take up the shield of faith and get ready to win!

How is my walk of faith? Is it producing results in my life?

_____
_____
_____
_____
_____
_____
_____
_____
_____
_____
_____
_____
_____
_____

Personal Notes/Reflection

Helmet of Salvation
Chapter 16

Salvation! Like me, many of you love to hear the word. It brings such a clear picture to mind of how lost we were before God saved us and gave us new life through a relationship with Jesus Christ. This new relationship has transformed and radically changed who we once were. Salvation has brought healing, deliverance, freedom, and hope to our hearts and minds. At various times, when I conduct interviews with those desiring to serve in the Kingdom, one of the first questions I ask a candidate is to share their salvation experience with me. I do this because I want to hear who they were before God entered their hearts and how their lives were changed. In relating their salvation experience, I can determine the depth of their love for God, and whether they have for gotten where they were when He found them, and how their lives have been changed and transformed by Him.

This is significant because you must remember where you were and how He delivered you. You are then able to share with those who are in need of salvation how God can change a life that is turned over to Him. Many of you have a simple salvation story of one day realizing you were lost and alone then you made the decision to invite God into your heart. Since He has come in, your life has been more peaceful, purposeful, and meaningful. There are others who have a more dramatic story of having been so lost in sin and devastation God had to move great mountains to rescue you before being destroyed by the enemy. Whatever your story, salvation is the door which guarantees you an eternity spent with the One who loves you enough to give you everything through the death of His beloved Son.

The helmet was the piece of the armor worn on the Roman soldiers' head during times of war. It was beautifully decorated and admired by all who saw it. A picture comes to mind each time I think about this elaborate headdress and how it stands out from all others. This picture is of the guards who stand at attention in front of the Queen's palace in England wearing this high headdress that covers most of their faces. It is impressive and makes the soldiers look dignified. The Roman soldier's helmet was strong, heavy, massive, and magnificently decorated with a colored plume standing tall and straight – very impressive. The Apostle Paul, under the guidance of the Holy Spirit, compares our salvation to this beautiful and impressive helmet. The picture he paints about salvation is the most beautiful, complex, amazing, wonderful, and impressive gift God ever gave to you and me. When you receive the gift of salvation and allow the Lord to change you, this brings a confidence and assurance to your life. Many people will notice the change in you. Salvation makes you stand out in a crowd just like the soldier's helmet because people will be able to see your life has been transformed; and, when difficulties arise, you are undaunted because you are safe under the protection of the Lord.

Salvation showcases the power of God in your life and causes people to wonder what is different about you. The boldness and confidence you gain when you embrace this free and wonderful gift of salvation, draws people to you. They find out about your Source of help and learn how you can remain steady and secure in the face of tragic situations. Just as the soldiers wore their helmets to protect their heads in battle, you must embrace your salvation so you will have security and assurance of your destination, as you prepare for eternity. Salvation keeps you from losing your peace, joy, and strength in the battles of life.

Have you ever seen people going through a crisis who do not have a relationship with the Lord? Have you wondered how they are able to endure without having God on their side? I have often wondered about this, and I pray for their salvation. It has taught me to be ready to share Christ with them since He is the only One who can deliver and set them free in a crisis. Put on the helmet of salvation to protect your mind from the enemy's lies, accusations, imaginations, and fears. The enemy uses your mind to plant seeds of destruction in your life. When you put on the helmet of salvation, the lies of sickness, lack, and fear will cease from harassing you because it protects and guards your mind. The helmet keeps the devil from accusing you. He tells you that you will never amount to anything, and your mental and emotional issues will keep you from winning. He is a liar, so send him packing! The helmet guards your mind from wrong imaginations. It keeps you from dwelling on the wrong things about your life. As a result, your imagination will not produce thoughts that will hurt, harm, or hinder you from being a blessing to yourself and others. It will create a place of peace, rest, safety, and joy – a haven for you. It is a place where you can create a life that you enjoy every day.

When Jesus died and provided salvation, not only did He want you to spend eternity with Him, but He also gave you much more. The word salvation is "sozo" in the Greek. Sozo means to save, heal, deliver, preserve, protect, make well, and make whole. Jesus came to save you so you will have eternal life. He also came to heal your emotions and your physical body. His death on the cross not only secured your eternal salvation but He bore your sicknesses and diseases, as well. Many years ago, I read there are thirty-nine root causes for all diseases in the world. Therefore, for each of those thirty-nine stripes Jesus bore on His back, He bore one for your healing. Jesus came to deliver you from everything that would keep you in bondage. Sin no longer has any power over you because it was rendered powerless on the cross of Calvary. You must stop allowing fear to torment you because the Bible says, "*Perfect love casts out fear* (1 John 4:18 NKJV)." God provided salvation to make you well and whole. When you are well, you are healthy, robust, strong, and full of life; and, when you are whole, you live in peace – body, mind, and spirit. Salvation completes you and keeps you from being broken and destroyed in battle. The helmet of salvation keeps your thoughts free and clear so you can achieve every assignment for the Kingdom of God. Remember to put on your helmet daily, by giving thanks to God for His amazing gift of salvation.

What is my salvation story?

_____

_____

_____

_____

_____

_____

_____

_____

_____

_____

_____

_____

_____

_____

_____

_____

How has becoming saved changed my life?

_____

_____

_____

_____

_____

_____

_____

_____

_____

_____

_____

_____

Personal Notes/Reflection

Shoes of Peace
Chapter 17

The offensive pieces of the armor are the pieces that place you in a position of courage and strength to face the enemy head on. When you are on the offensive, you are in the driver's seat; and you are in control of the situation with the devil on the run. Unfortunately, when the enemy attacks, you are often on the run from him. He comes at you with many hurtful and devastating situations, and you find yourself backing up and running for cover. He will often back you into a corner making you think you have no way out. It may seem as if you have no defense against him, but that is a lie. He uses smoke screens because he knows you have many tools in your arsenal which, if used properly, will do severe damage to him and his kingdom. To be on the offensive means you are on the attack. You go into his territory demanding he return, without delay, the things he has stolen from you, in Je sus' name. Your position of attack lets him know you will not sit idly by and allow him to do untold damage in your life. In the offensive position, you are the aggressor not waiting around to see what he will bring against you. You are taking a stance by putting on your weapons of warfare and demonstrating you have everything in your arsenal to win, because Jesus gave them to you. When you understand what you have been given, you can stand secure and surefooted knowing you have the victory. You will discover that the greater One lives in you, and He has given you the power to overcome and to be victorious in every battle (1 John 4:4).

God has given you offensive pieces of the armor that provide steadfastness in the battles. He has provided you shoes of peace, a sword, and prayer, which are powerful weapons of war. As you explore these remarkable weapons, ask God to give you the tenacity as you take hold of each one, and use them effectively in your everyday life. Now, let us begin our exploration of these weapons.

...and with your feet fitted with the readiness that comes from the gospel of peace. Ephesians 6:15 (NIV)

In this scripture, the Apostle Paul talks to you about dressing yourself with the shoes of peace. He used the shoes the Roman soldiers wore in battle to paint a vivid picture of what God has in store for you, as you begin to walk in peace. The soldier's shoes had deadly force, and they were vicious weapons that could do untold damage to their enemies in battle. The shoes were specially made with metal and had sharp dangerous spikes protruding from the bottom. The inventor of those shoes had a plan in mind when he designed them. The plan was to keep the soldiers secure and stable as they fought to win. The spikes at the bottom of the shoes kept the soldiers steady during the fight. In close combat, the soldiers would give one deadly kick with those spiked shoes.

The Apostle Paul uses this lethal weapon to connect you to your peace. Your peace is a deadly weapon, which you can use very effectively against the devil; and when the peace of God is in full operation in your life, you will always win because the enemy will not move you. God's peace protects and defends you from the assaults of the evil one, and His peace keeps you marching forward in the battle by giving you rest in whatever state you are in. Just as the soldiers' shoes kept them steady in war, the peace of God will keep you steady and prepared for battle. His peace will keep the enemy from overcoming you in battle.

How do I stay steady and secure during the battle?

_____

_____

_____

_____

_____

_____

_____

_____

_____

Many of you have found yourselves in crisis situations where you asked for, and believed you received His peace, but your heart was still not settled. During a storm that affected the Texas region, many people were worried and afraid for their lives and their properties. In conversations before, during, and after the storm, I learned the fear of dying in the storm almost caused people's hearts to fail them. They prayed for the peace of God, and confessed they had the supernatural peace that passes all understanding to keep their hearts and minds through Christ Jesus (Philippians 4:7); but their hearts refused to be comforted. The words were spoken, they knew what the Word said, but for some reason those words were not keeping them steady and in peace during the storm.

It is important to know the Word of God is your provision to give you life, and life more abundantly (John 10:10). You and I must take the Word from the realm of just believing, to a place of knowing without a doubt the Word is true, and it has power to change our lives. You must take the seeds of the Word from your mind and make sure those seeds are deeply planted into the soil of your heart. For the Word to be effective and powerful in your life, you must believe it, and also know it is the truth. It is to be embraced not only in your mind, but in your heart, as well. The Word must take up permanent residency in your heart so it can work for you when you need it. Although the people confessed the Word during the storm, it was only head knowledge, not heart knowledge.
That is why they experienced the fear that almost caused their hearts to fail.

You must bind the Word of God and the peace of God into your heart, mind, and emotions. The Prophet Isaiah explains very clearly that the way to do this is to steadfastly keep your mind on God and the truth of His Word. Isaiah 26:3 (NKJV) – "*You will keep him in perfect peace, whose mind is stayed on You, because he trusts in You.*" It is the peace from the Word of God that will keep you stable in the storms. It will fortify you, strengthen you, comfort you, give you hope, and keep you steady when devastating circumstances occur in your life.

Thank God for His peace daily, and don't settle for the peace you had yesterday. You need His peace every day to bring you through any challenges you face. Be prepared and ready for war by making sure you have the assurance of His peace operating in your life. Peace empowers you to conquer the enemy, and it is your protection from the fiery darts that the enemy shoots at you. Peace guards your heart and mind; and gives you amazing rest in warfare. Peace during the battle will let others see you are not alone, someone guides you, holds you, and keeps you standing in faith. Peace, peace, peace – receive it and never let it go.

Your peace position is:
- Having done all, stand.
- Let the peace of God rule your heart.
- The peace of God will guard your heart and mind in Christ Jesus.
- You are the bearer of peace to all people.
- God desires that you overflow daily with His peace.

What fear has kept my heart from being at peace?

_____

_____

_____

_____

_____

_____

_____

_____

_____

_____

Personal Notes/Reflection

Sword of the Spirit
Chapter 18

...and the sword of the spirit, which is the word of God. Ephesians 6:17b (NIV)

When I hear the word sword, I instantly think of duels, battles, fighting, and the strong possibility of death to an opponent. The sword is a lethal weapon. In the hand of the right person, a sword is powerful, effective, and assures that you always have the victory. The Roman soldier's sword was such a weapon and could cause serious damage to the enemy. The sword, about 19 inches long, was razor sharp on both sides, with a tip that turned upwards and resembled a corkscrew. Because it was razor sharp, the soldiers could cut the enemy to pieces. It was used in hand-to-hand combat. This weapon was the deadliest sword the Roman soldiers had during their time, and it brought terror to the imagination. Using this weapon, the soldiers engaged in up close and personal fights with their opponents. This one-on-one combat meant the enemy was fighting and was focused on only one soldier in the midst of all the other fighting going on around them, and it was a fight to the death.

The Apostle Paul is saying God has given the believer a weapon that is frightening to the devil and his forces. It is horrific to them because it does untold damage. The weapon given to you by God is His Word. God has given you the "logos," which is Greek for His written Word. As you meditate on the Word day and night (Joshua 1:8), the Word will change your mind, your heart, and eventually your life. The written Word is filled with power and wisdom. Though the logos (written word), is powerful, Paul is not speaking specifically about the logos, the written Word, when he talks about the sword of the spirit. He is talking about the "rhema word" – the living, active word which is sharper than any two-edged sword, penetrating even to dividing soul and spirit, joints and marrow; it judges the thoughts and the attitudes of the heart (Heb. 4:12). The rhema word is a specific word God gives to you during a crisis or a difficult situation.

When sickness comes upon you, out of hundreds of scriptures in the Bible, God may give you just one or two to stand on and to confess daily. As you spend time with Him meditating on His Word, it will illuminate your mind, heart, and life. God gives you His Word during your sickness. He says to you, "Who forgives all your sins and heals all your diseases (Psalm 103:3). He sent His Word and healed them (Psalm 107:20). By His stripes I am healed (Isaiah 53:5)." As He speaks these words to your heart, He is giving you a specific word for your situation.

When you read the Word, meditate on it. When you begin to speak it, the scripture registers in your mind and brings courage, confidence, and healing to your body. This specific word for your life comes directly from the mouth of God to your heart.

Rick Renner, in his book *Sparkling Gems from the Greek*, explains it beautifully. He says the rhema word that God speaks to your heart becomes a double-edged sword for you to use to counteract the attack of the enemy. When God speaks a word over your life, one side of the sword is manifested. When you receive, then speak the same word God has spoken to your heart, the other side of the sword comes into play the double-edged sword. Let me re peat that one side of the sword comes out of God's mouth when He speaks a specific word to you; and, as you speak the exact word God has spoken to you over your situation, you bring the other edge of the sword into existence. This is a powerful example of how vitally important the Word is for your life as you seek to be the victor in the battles. The double-edged sword always works.

Hebrews 4:12 tells us how the sword works. The sword, the Word, is living. It is alive! Because it is alive, it contains power. The Word is active, it has energy, it has vigor, and is filled with spirit. The Word is sharp, and it cuts deeply. This same Word penetrates your soul and searches out the intentions of your heart. The Word sheds light about what is going on in your soul and the private chambers of your heart. It is God's Word that judges your thoughts and clarifies the attitudes that have taken root in your heart. His Word shows you what is in your heart toward Him and toward others.

Someone defined logos – the written Word of God as the "said word," it has been spoken and it will not change. No one can change God's written Word it is everlasting and true. The rhema word is defined as the "saying word" of God. This means the Word is continually spoken over your situation which is why the Bible says it is alive, powerful, and active. It is on the move, never stopping, and it is working daily to help you live your life victoriously.

We find an example of the rhema word at work in Matthew chapter four, when Jesus called the disciples. Jesus went walking by the Sea of Galilee with a purpose in mind. He knew He would encounter those whom God had assigned to help Him in His earthly ministry. As He walked, he saw two brothers, Simon called Peter and his brother Andrew. They were fishing and Jesus said to them, "*Come, follow Me and I will make you fishers of men.*" Jesus called and commissioned them to no longer fish to satisfy man's natural hunger; they were to fish to satisfy the hunger and longing in the souls of men.

Jesus selected them for a higher calling; and this calling was to bring man eternal life through Him. Jesus knew they would respond to His call because God had already done the work of preparing their hearts. They received, and then responded to the word of life they heard from the voice of Jesus. Without hesitation, they moved out on the rhema word – '*come follow me*'.

Jesus continued His walk and came across two more brothers who were in a boat with their father, Zebedee. He called James and John who instantly left the boat and their father, to follow Him. I want you to see how powerful the rhema word is. These four men chose to follow a stranger. They walked away from their work, their families, and their livelihood to follow the voice of someone who simply said, "*Come and follow Me.*" The rhema word was alive, active, and powerful; and it worked in their lives to produce the results of obedience and a willingness to leave all they had to follow Jesus.

As you read further in the book of Matthew, you come to another powerful example of the rhema word at work in the life of the Apostle Peter. Jesus finished ministering to a group of people and after He dismissed them, He went up the mountain to pray. In the middle of the night, Jesus decided to join His disciples; but since He had no boat, He began to walk towards them on the water. When the disciples saw Him walking on the water, they were terrified and thought it was a ghost. In fear, they cried out. Jesus comforted them by saying, "*It is I.*" He admonished them to take courage and not be afraid. Peter heard His voice but wanted more proof. Peter said to Jesus, "*Lord, if it's You, tell me to come to You on the water.*" He called Jesus, Lord, meaning master, which means his heart knew it was Jesus, but his mind was not receiving nor accepting the message that it was Him. Jesus said one word, "*Come.*" It was the same word He had previously used when He called them to follow Him. He simply told them to "come", and they came. When Peter heard the word "come," he stepped out of the boat and directly onto the water, on the spoken word. In that instant, he did not consider that man is not able to walk on water without sinking and drowning. He heard the word, and he went. He began walking toward Jesus based on the rhema word he had received. This was a specific word given only to Peter because He asked it of the Lord. No one else in the boat asked Jesus to allow him to walk on the water, and they were wise to stay put in the boat. If anyone other than Peter had stepped out on the rhema word, it would not have worked for him. It was a specific word given to Peter, directly from Jesus.

Your rhema word from God will do serious damage to the devil because it is like the dagger the soldiers used to kill their enemies in war. This is the dagger you use to plunge into the devil's heart to bring about his defeat. Your words have life and can create a bright future for you depending on how you use them, or your words can demolish your dreams. The sword of the spirit – the powerful Word of God will take you from defeat to victory in every situation. Remember to use it and watch how powerfully it will work for you.

How has the Word of God been effective in my life?

_____

_____

_____

_____

What specific scriptures has God given me to help me face crisis situations?

_____
_____
_____
_____
_____
_____
_____
_____
_____
_____
_____
_____
_____
_____
_____
_____
_____
_____

Personal Notes/Reflection

Armor of Prayer
Chapter 19

And pray in the Spirit on all occasions with all kinds of prayers and requests. With this in mind, be alert and always keep on praying for all the saints. Ephesians 6:18 (NIV)

Let us begin by exploring some wonderful keys, insight, and wisdom about prayer. Get ready to embrace some amazing changes in your circumstances, as you make prayer paramount in your life.

What is Prayer?

Be joyful always; pray continually; give thanks in all circumstances, for this is God's will for you in Christ Jesus 1 Thessalonians 5:1618 (NIV)

The word prayer is used approximately one hundred and twenty-seven times in the New Testament. This is a clear indication of how important prayer is to your life. Prayer means coming face-to-face with God and suggests an intimate contact. Prayer brings you up close and personal with God and gives you an opportunity to meet Him on a level of intimacy you will not encounter with Him in any other way.

When you pray, you express your desires, wishes, hopes, and vows to God. The Greeks de fined prayer as a vow. They call it a votive offering which is like a pledge you make to God about your intentions. When you pray, you come face-to-face with God; and, as you encounter Him, you will never leave His presence the same. Prayer, you will discover, is a place of sacrifice, a place of decision, a place of consecration, and a place where you make and then honor your vows. The sacrifice comes into play because your one focus is God. You must discipline yourself to be still and often remain silent so you can hear Him. You sacrifice your desire to always do the talking, and you submit yourself to be still and listen for the voice of God. When you begin praying and petitioning God about your needs, you will never leave His presence empty handed. If you have experienced times when you prayed and you were not encouraged, refreshed, restored, renewed, or given an answer, I can say from experience you did not wait and listen long enough for God's response. God will never be silent when you seek Him in prayer.

Prayer is also a place of consecration because your will and your desires are given over to God so you can seek His will and plans for you. When you consecrate your life to God, you dedicate and devote your all to Him and seek His desires for you. In consecrating yourself to Him, you seal your commitment and your dedication to His ways of doing things. Prayer is a place of decision.

Decide to leave everything in God's presence, because only He can handle it and help you to overcome.

Over the years I have heard a variety of concerns while ministering to people. There are those who have struggled with parents, sons, daughters, aunts, uncles, etc. and have fervently prayed for God to intervene and help them in their struggles. Problems arise because they have prayed for God's help, but they want God to do it their way. They do not necessarily want their loved ones to go through any difficulties or suffering to gain wisdom to make better life decisions. They desire God's help, but they don't want Him to handle it His way. When you pray seeking God's help, decide God knows best, and leave the situation in His hands. As you understand He loves your family, children, and spouse more than you could possibly love them, you will know their eternal salvation is most important to Him. Sometimes people are so willful in their choices it may take something major, or even catastrophic, to get them to a point of repentance and turning to God for help. Some people must hit rock bottom before they are willing to look up and acknowledge their need for God. Therefore, decide to leave the outcome to God, and trust Him when you pray. Do not tell Him how to do things since He will always do it His way. You must surrender your will in exchange for His.

When you engage in prayer, you are in communion with God, and this is where you develop trust, confidence, and faith in His ability to help you. Prayer is a channel for God to pour His power through you and unlock His power in your life. Praying gives you power to overcome doubt, fear, defeat, and it keeps you from being overwhelmed in the battle. Prayer is an amazing adventure. When you go into prayer, you may not immediately know for what or whom God would have you to pray. I discovered this adventure many years ago, which has since changed my dread of prayer into a love of praying.

Prayer is a necessity for your life. It is not a mechanical act or a formula you follow, but it flows out of a heart filled with love and needs that only God can supply. In surrendering your will to God, you come to understand that God not only wants to bless you, but He wants to change your heart and your life. When you exchange your will and desires for His, He will touch and change you by His power and presence. Having an attitude of thanksgiving during prayer demonstrates you will wait in faith, and expectancy, until the manifestation comes. As you wait in faith, expect God to move at any time but not necessarily how and when you decide He should move. Look for the unexpected around every corner!

Luke chapter eleven gives us some keys about how to develop and have an effective prayer life. The word says one day Jesus was praying in a certain place; and, when He finished, one of His disciples said to Him, "Lord, teach us to pray, just as John taught His disciples." He said to them, "When you pray, say, "Our Father which art in heaven, hallowed be Thy name. Thy kingdom come, Thy will be done on earth as it is in heaven. Give us this day our daily bread, and forgive us our sins, for we also forgive every one that is indebted to us. And lead us not into temptation but deliver us from evil."

In this passage of scripture, Jesus gives us a formula for praying effectively

Prayer Formula (7 P's for praying)

1. We must find a *place* to commune with Him – a quiet place where we can experience Him without distractions.
2. He teaches us how to enter His *presence*. We should posture ourselves in such a way that we respect, honor, and reverence Him.
3. He then tells us there are certain *priorities* when we pray. The first priority is to desire to see His will done on earth as it is being done in heaven.
4. He promises us *provision* each time we seek Him. He plans to meet our daily needs.
5. He gives us permission to pray for the needs of *people* so they will be blessed.
6. He shows us, as we pray, *power* is released into our lives so it can flow through us to impact the lives of others.
7. He reminds us the proper way to enter His presence is to praise Him, and give Him thanks for all He has been to us and done for us.

What things do I do when I pray to bring God's presence in my life?

_____

_____

_____

_____

_____

_____

_____

_____

_____

_____

How to Release God's Power and Presence in Prayer

When you ask, you do not receive, because you ask with wrong motives, that you may spend what you get on your pleasures. James 4:3 (NIV)

The power and presence of God is released into your life when you know how to ask for the right things. James chapter four says you ask amiss and with the wrong motives. This means you are asking for wrong and inappropriate things; things that are not in agreement with God's will for you. There are, however, times when you do ask according to His will, but fear, doubt, and unbelief cancel out your requests. It is important to know what to ask God for in prayer and how to ask so you receive the petitions you desire from Him.

Approach God with confidence and boldly enter His presence knowing you are welcomed as His son or daughter. When you understand the promises revealed in the Bible are His plans for you; and, as you begin to pray for those things, you will get results. The Bible promises God always hears and grants the petitions you ask of Him when it is in line with His will for you.

You were designed by God with the ability to know and understand His plans for your life. He ratified His plans by sending Jesus to the cross so you could be victorious. When you accepted Jesus and the Holy Spirit came to live in your heart, you received a deposit of power. You now reside in the Son of God, and He now resides in you. The miracle working power that raised Jesus from the dead has taken up residence in your heart.

Scripture tells how deeply concerned God is about you. He knows the number of hairs on your head, even those you have lost (Matthew 10:30). To receive a release of His power and presence in your prayer life, you must be convinced and confident when you pray and seek Him; and He will show up in your situation. God is all knowing and powerful, and His power is available to you. He has the power to do anything, to change anyone, and to step in and intervene when no one else can make a difference for you.

In what ways is God's power operating in my life?

_____

_____

_____

_____

_____

_____

How to Clearly Hear from God

And the word of the Lord came to him: "What are you doing here, Elijah?" He replied, "I have been very zealous for the Lord God Almighty. The Israelites have rejected your covenant, bro ken down your altars, and put your prophets to death with the sword. I am the only one left, and now they are trying to kill me too." The Lord said, "Go out and stand on the mountain in the presence of the Lord, for the Lord is about to pass by." Then a great and powerful wind tore the mountains apart and shattered the rocks before the Lord, but the Lord was not in the wind. After the wind there was an earthquake, but the Lord was not in the earthquake. After the earthquake came a fire, but the Lord was not in the fire. And after the fire came a gentle whisper. When Elijah heard it, he pulled his cloak over his face and went out and stood at the mouth of the cave.

1 King 19:9b13 (NIV)

Hearing God clearly is key to having a fulfilling prayer life. There are many ways you hear the voice of the Lord. You hear Him through His written Word, through the Holy Spirit's still small voice in your heart, and God will also speak through the voice of concerned friends and loved ones. When you encounter difficulties, God is often speaking. When you are convicted by your wrong choices, God is speaking. When you are corrected through the Word or through other people, God is speaking. Joel 2:28-29 says God speaks through our dreams and visions. God can also speak through a prophetic word containing instructions for your life. Usually, the prophetic word is a confirming word He has already shared with you. Scripture says to test every word you are given against the Word of God to ascertain whether God is speaking to you. God will also speak through the storms, earthquakes, disasters, and other tragic events. The key is to listen for His voice. The above passage of scripture shows us God speaks in many ways.

When God decided to speak to Elijah, he did not hear the voice of God in the powerful wind, nor in the earthquake, or the fire. Elijah heard the voice of God in a gentle whisper. Be careful you do not disregard what you are seeing, hearing, and reading. God is intent on getting His message to you. He will deliver it in many different ways to catch your attention, so you do not miss what He has planned for your life.

Let me clarify some things for you:

- God is always speaking to you.
- He never stops reaching out to you.
- You belong to Him, and He will always communicate with you.
- His voice is not the voice of a stranger to His children.
- You must wait, listen, hear, and then obey His voice.
- Stop questioning if it is your imagination instead of the voice of God.
- Know that most of the time when you hear Him, it will be through the sound of your own voice, or an inner knowing.

121

Causes for Ineffective Prayers

There are many reasons you do not hear God clearly, and why your prayers may be ineffective. A lack of focus when you pray will keep you from effective communication and reception. Many of you are easily distracted while you are praying, or you may feel unworthy to ask anything of the Lord. At other times, you may be blocked by the enemy's attacks. Distance yourself from distractions and concentrate when praying to get to the heart of the issues you face. Make God your focal point as you seek Him for answers. In Mark chapter nine, Jesus took His three closest disciples Peter, James, and John to a high mountain where He was transfigured before their eyes. Elijah and Moses appeared and talked with Jesus. Seeing this, Peter boldly spoke up and told Jesus it was good they were with Him and announced they should put up three memorial stones to commemorate this event. As Peter said this, God spoke from heaven and told them "This is my Son, listen to Him!" When they looked again, they only saw Jesus. It is apparent Peter's statement was not appropriate or even timely, therefore, his request was not granted.

Why was Peter's statement inappropriate? It was because he was speaking when he should have been listening, learning, and gaining wisdom from this powerful move of God. God was demonstrating His power in their midst and making it clear that Jesus was His Son. This was a time of reverence and worship, and it should have produced humility in the hearts of the disciples, because Jesus had invited them to this special encounter with His Father. I think Peter spoke up because he was so awed and simply did not know what else to do.

When God visits you in an amazing way, choose to remain quiet and still so you do not miss anything He wants to impart to you. Many of you have also experienced times when your requests were not granted; and these times can be extremely difficult. It is important to know what to ask for when you pray and be sure you are not asking God for inappropriate things. As Jesus and the three disciples came down the mountain, they met the other disciples who were surrounded by a large crowd arguing with the teachers of the law. Jesus asked them what they were arguing about, and a man told Him he had brought his son, who was demon possessed and in horrible pain, and the disciples were not able to cast the spirit out. Jesus spoke to them about their unbelief and asked that the boy be brought to Him. He asked the father about the boy's condition and the father said, "If you can do anything, take pity on us and help us."

As I read this story, it is clear this man came to Jesus not believing He was able to deliver his son; but he must have heard about Jesus delivering others. Although he was not quite sure if the same thing could happen for his son, in his desperation, he said to Jesus, "If You can…." How many times have you gone to Jesus just like this man doubting that He can change your situation? Jesus had the solution for him and for you. He said, "Everything is possible for him who believes (Mark 9:23 NIV)." He did not say a few things are possible, nor did He say some things are possible; He said everything is possible because He makes all things possible for those who choose to believe Him. The man made a profound statement by telling Jesus he believed, and then asking Jesus to help him overcome his unbelief. That seems contradictory. How could he believe but still need help with unbelief? This happens because people often waiver, not in their hearts, but in their minds. Their heart knows exactly what Jesus can do, but their mind keeps questioning whether He is able to perform miracles for them.

Prayers are often ineffective because of the various reasons listed above and for other personal reasons God reveals to you during your prayer time. If you are persistent and consistent in your prayer life, you will hear from God and receive a breakthrough. Give God the first part of your day, because He wants to begin each day with you. When you enter His presence, you set the tone not only for the day, but also for your life. You will develop an effective prayer life that will produce amazing results.

What is causing my prayers to be ineffective?

_____

_____

_____

_____

_____

_____

Dealing with Unanswered Prayers

Then the mother of Zebedee's sons came to Jesus with her sons and, kneeling down, asked a favor of him. "What is it you want?" he asked. She said, "Grant that one of these two sons of mine may sit at your right and the other at your left in your kingdom." "You don't know what you are asking," Jesus said to them. "Can you drink the cup I am going to drink?" "We can," they answered. Jesus said to them, "You will indeed drink from my cup, but to sit at my right or left is not for me to grant. These places belong to those for whom they have been prepared by my Father." Matthew 20:2023 (NIV)

There are people who have experienced, or will experience, deep hurt because they feel their prayers go unanswered. Often, they do not understand the reason for this. You think God is not listening, or He may not be concerned about the things that concern you. Some of you may feel God does not hear you when you pray because He is too busy to listen and grant your requests. When you pray, check your requests to determine if what you are asking of God is an appropriate request. Are you praying in agreement with God's will? Maybe you are asking God for wrong things or asking God to manipulate someone to accommodate your purpose.

Many times, we pray for the wrong things at the wrong time which is often the reason we do not receive the answers we are seeking from the Lord. Analyze your prayer requests to see if they will bring glory to God or, if they will only glorify you. Ask yourself "Am I making demands of God with the wrong attitude or motive?"

In the scripture mentioned above, the mother of those two brothers was audacious in asking Jesus for a favor; but she was looking out for the future of her sons. She knew Jesus had other disciples but wanted her sons to rule and reign closely with Him when He ascended His throne. She probably thought Jesus was ready to set up His kingdom on the earth and was expecting Jesus to establish His earthly kingdom during her lifetime. She had no idea the sufferings and hardship Jesus would endure to redeem her, her sons, and mankind. If this mother knew Jesus would not reign on earth until thousands of years later, and how He and her sons would suffer severe persecution and then horrible deaths, she would not have approached Him asking for this favor. It is apparent her request was inappropriate because Jesus told her God had already determined who would sit in which position next to His throne. this decision was the Father's alone. You may be asking God for the wrong things for your life, and this may be the reason you have not received an answer. God knows what is best for you, and He is looking out for your best interest. He keeps you away from harm and danger.

At times, your prayers may go unanswered or be hindered because of unconfessed sins, unforgiveness, bitterness, and even resentment, not only toward others but also toward God. These are barriers to being heard and receiving what God has reserved for you. A lack of trust, confidence, and faith in a loving God, who has only the best in mind for you, will also keep you from receiving what you are praying for. When you experience times God is not answering your prayers, do not turn away from Him. Press in and keep seeking Him, because He will answer those prayers and bless your life and bring glory to Himself.

In the book of Daniel, there is an example of how to wait for God's answers in your life. One day, while Daniel was praying and studying, he received a revelation that Jerusalem was going to be desolate for approximately seventy years, and he sought God's help for himself and his people, God responded by giving him a vision of a great war. Daniel fasted for twenty-one days praying, mourning, and seeking the face of the Lord. Three weeks after seeking and praying, an angel finally appeared to him. The angel told him the moment He prayed, God had heard him and sent the answer. The answer had been delayed for twenty-one days because the prince, (high demon) of the Persian kingdom delayed and resisted him from bringing the answer to Daniel. God had to send Michael, another angel to help get the answer to Daniel. This delay was not because God did not answer immediately but it was an attempt by the enemy to keep the answer from Daniel. As he waited, Daniel kept the right attitude, and his attitude while waiting is worth sharing:

- He had humility while waiting.
- He did not develop an attitude with God and walk away from Him in frustration.
- He had an attitude of fear (awe) and reverence for God as He waited.
- He trusted, even though the answer was delayed.
- He fasted as he waited; he wanted to get self out of the way so he could hear God clearly.
- He persisted in prayer, he never stopped.
- He worshipped God, reminding Him, He was great and awesome.
- He reminded God about His covenant of love to His people.
- He confessed not only his sins but also the sins of all the people. He covered every possible area that might block his prayers.
- He asked God to be merciful and forgiving to a people who rebelled against Him.
- He then rested in God.
- Daniel understood the answers could only be found in the presence and person of God, and he simply prayed, trusted, and waited on Him.

What has been my attitude while waiting for the answers?

_____

_____

_____

_____

_____

_____

_____

_____

_____

_____

_____

Praying Mountain Moving Prayers

In the morning, as they went along, they saw the fig tree withered from the roots. Peter remembered and said to Jesus, "Rabbi, look! The fig tree you cursed has withered!" "Have faith in God," Jesus answered. "I tell you the truth, if anyone says to this mountain, 'Go, throw yourself into the sea,' and does not doubt in his heart but believes that what he says will happen, it will be done for him." Mark 11:2023 (NIV)

The prayer armor God has given you can move the mountains of difficulties and devastation from your life, as you learn to pray. In order for you to pray mountain moving prayers, you must know the Word of God; know Jesus, the living Word, and get to know the Bible (the logos), the written Word of God. God's Word is like a mustard seed you plant deeply into the soil of your heart. It will produce a harvest in your life, as you nurture and develop it.

The Word is powerful and life changing. God says heaven and earth will pass away but His Word will never pass away (Luke 21:33 & Mark 13:31). This powerful, alive, and active Word also searches out your heart, and the intentions of your heart, so your motives are always pure, when you pray.

Jesus made a profound statement to the devil while He was being tested and tempted in the wilderness. He told the devil man shall not live by bread alone, but by every word that comes out of the mouth of God (Matthew 4:4). You and I can survive without bread, but we will suffer without the Word of God operating in our lives. The Word has sustaining power to keep you during the battle. Jeremiah, chapter one, says God will hasten His Word to perform it in your life. God will not hasten your pleading, crying, emotional outburst or even what you are hoping He will do for you, but He will hasten His Word, and He will work based on His Word alone. Speaking the Word of God over your life will bring untold blessings.

In John, chapter eleven, there is a beautiful example of how the Word of God is so powerful. One of Jesus' great friends, Lazarus, died and Mary and Martha, Lazarus' sisters, summoned Jesus but He delayed His arrival for several days. It was a Jewish practice to bury their dead within twenty-four hours, but it was believed that up to the third day there was a possibility life could be restored to the body because the spirit hovered for three days after death. Jesus, in His wisdom, delayed His arrival until the fourth day when there was no chance the spirit could be returned to the body, as they had believed. He wanted to make sure they knew, without a doubt, this miracle was from God. When He arrived, He was taken to the tomb and was told by Martha that her brother Lazarus already smelled because He had been buried for four days. Jesus heard her, but He was on an assignment to bring glory to God, and the people needed to see a demonstration that He was indeed God's Son. Jesus did something simple but profound after praying, He used words and spoke to Lazarus' dead body saying, "Lazarus, come forth." When Lazarus heard the words, he came out of the grave wrapped in grave clothing. He was resurrected and given new life by the spoken words of Jesus and by the authority that was inherent in those words.

When you use God's Word correctly and with authority, it has power to radically change you. You can speak to dead things in your life like dreams, sickness, financial lack, loneliness, or whatever is holding you captive and they must obey you. The power and authority of the Word will bring resurrection life to your situation.

What are my greatest needs? Write a prayer confession using the example on the next page.

_____

_____

_____

_____

_____

_____

_____

_____

_____

_____

_____

_____

_____

_____

_____

Example of Praying the Word

Father, in the name of Jesus, I (insert your name) thank You for the job or new position you have prepared for my life. Psalm 1:3 says I am like a tree planted by the rivers of water that bears its fruit in season, my leaves shall not wither and whatever I do shall prosper. Psalm 2:8 says for me to ask You, and You will make the nations my inheritance and the ends of the earth my possession, therefore, I thank You that You have hand selected the right job or position for me. I confess Romans 4:20 which says I do not waiver in unbelief at God's promise, but I am strengthened in my faith and give glory to God for all the good things He does in my life. Mark 11:24 says all the things I pray and ask for; I must believe I have received them, and I will have them. I thank You for the great job and promotion You are bringing into my life, and it will go beyond what I can think or imagine.

Father, Psalm 18:32 says You clothe me with strength and make my way perfect. I thank you based on Psalm 20:4, You will give me what my heart desires and fulfill Your purpose in me. I also thank You that Psalm 25:3a says not one person who waits on You will be disgraced. I take Your Word as my medicine and wait with expectancy for its fulfillment in my life.

Amen!

Personal Notes/Reflection

Victory!

Victory in the Midst of the Battle
Chapter 20

Victory! This is a word filled with hope for you who have been in a battle and need to be rescued. When you hear the word victory, it should recall a picture of deliverance and freedom. Victory means to be a victor, a champion, a winner, and a conqueror, to celebrate, to accomplish, to succeed, and to rejoice. It should give you a picture of always coming out on top. It speaks of having been in a struggle and then being crowned the victor. It means you win, and you have learned how to conquer those who are trying to overcome you. You have reason to celebrate when you are in the winners' circle, because you have accomplished what was set before you and have been successful in your mission.

There are rewards for the trials and tribulations you have endured and overcome, and you will receive the rewards for having fought well and for being steadfast in the midst of the battle. You will be compensated for the battles! Payday is coming and you will gain and retain a crown of righteousness because Jesus paid the ultimate price for your success. The prize will be your medal, a badge of honor, which signifies you have the privilege and the advantage over the enemy. Some of you will receive financial rewards, others will regain health, others will see relationships restored, and some will see restoration of family members who were once astray brought back into the fold because you stayed the course to win the prize. You have the advantage in the battle! Jesus has given this advantage to you. Let us look at what God does for you when you go into battle.

He said: "Listen, King Jehoshaphat and all who live in Judah and Jerusalem! This is what the Lord says to you: 'Do not be afraid or discouraged because of this vast army. For the battle is not yours, but God's. Tomorrow march down against them. They will be climbing up by the Pass of Ziz, and you will find them at the end of the gorge in the Desert of Jeruel. You will not have to fight this battle. Take up your positions; stand firm and see the deliverance the Lord will give you, O Judah and Jerusalem. Do not be afraid; do not be discouraged. Go out to face them tomorrow, and the Lord will be with you." 2 Chronicles 20:1517 (NIV)

This scripture paints a vivid picture of how God fights for you. King Jehoshaphat received word the Moabites and Ammonites were coming to war against him. When he heard the news, he was afraid and went into prayer to seek answers from the Lord. He also declared a fast for himself and the people to be certain they would clearly hear the voice of the Lord. He gathered all the people around him to unify them as a nation and to connect them with God. Jehoshaphat understood there was power in unity.

When he gathered all the people, he began praying and reminding God of who He was, and of His promises to His people. He reminded God He was ruler, and all power was in His hands. He also told God when troubles, battles, and calamities came, they would stand in His presence before the temple that bears His Name, and they would cry out to Him in their distress, and He would hear them. The king understood he did not stand a chance of winning this battle in his own strength, power and might, so he went to the only One who could bring deliverance. He told God they did not know what to do, but their eyes were fixed on Him. In effect, he said, "God, if you don't look down from heaven, see our distress, and come to our rescue, we will be annihilated." He understood only the power of God could sustain them in the battle, and God answered their cry.

What does it mean to me to walk in unity?

_____
_____
_____
_____
_____
_____
_____
_____

How has walking in unity with others been beneficial to my life?

_____
_____
_____
_____
_____
_____
_____
_____
_____
_____
_____
_____
_____

God sent a word of encouragement to the King and the people. He told them not to fear and gave them the greatest news they could have ever heard – "The battle is not yours, but God's." God is saying the same thing to you during your battles. He is telling you sickness, lack of resources, trouble in your marriage, the wrong choices your children are making, which are devastating to you, are battles you cannot fight on your own. He has made them His battles; He will fight them for you, and He will always win.

The king and the people heard the words, were encouraged in their hearts, and confident they were fully covered in the battle. God gave them some instructions. *First,* they had to take up their position, as He directed. *Second,* they were to stand firm, watch God work, and then behold His deliverance. *Third,* He exhorted them again not to be afraid but to remain encouraged. *Fourth,* they were to go out and face the enemy, and He would be with them. What God was really saying was this battle was a piece of cake for Him, so He wanted them to have front row seats to watch Him at work. God gave them additional instructions about what to do to guarantee their success. Jehoshaphat appointed men to sing to the Lord and praise Him for the splendor of His holiness. He placed the praise singers at the head of the battle. As they began to sing, God showed up and the armies began destroying themselves.

When the king and the people arrived at the lookout point all they saw were dead bodies. Jehoshaphat and His men did not have to fight; they simply walked into the camp and carried off the spoils from the battle. The victory God won for them was so complete it took the men three days to gather up all the goods from the enemy. Not only will God fight and win for you, but He will also make the enemy pay you for all the stress, worry, and fear he brings into your life.

What victories has God given me?

_____
_____
_____
_____
_____
_____
_____
_____
_____
_____
_____
_____
_____

There is a prize you will gain after the battle; all you need to do is follow God's instructions and then go in and gather the rewards. You are a victor because the conqueror Himself lives in you. When you grasp this truth, you will understand the devil is no match for you when God is backing you. You are more than a conqueror because you are over, above, and beyond the devil's reach; and since God is for you, who dares go against you. Jesus stripped the enemy of his power over you and left him naked, powerless, and exposed. He dethroned him and put him on display for all to see. God stands guard over you, ready to fight for you and to win every time.

What prize(s) do you desire from the Lord?

_____

_____

_____

_____

_____

How to Attain Victory in the Battle

In chapter two of this book, we talked about the battles in which you are involved. A few things in that chapter bear repeating. Remember, you are engaged in a battle that has been raging for centuries. The enemy's attacks have increased against you because he knows his time is running out. You must be alert, aware, and armed to defeat him to be victorious in the battle you are fighting. Most of his attacks are subtle. Your mind and emotions are attacked, but other times it is a full-scale war against your health, your finances, and your family.

Satan has lied, deceived, murdered, slandered, and stolen from you. He has accused you before God and others and has tried his best to tempt you away from God's protection so he can bring devastation to your life. He seems to have forgotten that Jesus already won the victory for you at Calvary. John 1:5 (KJV) says, "*The light shineth in darkness; and the darkness comprehended it not.*" This scripture is telling you darkness does not have the ability to sup press or hold your light under its authority. The devil, who is darkness, may try to overcome the light; but he will not succeed against you. He will be frustrated in his attempts because God will always prevail, so he cannot put out your light or gain victory over you. You have been fortified with power to win and to maintain a winning position in life. Let us explore some of your winning strategies.

Praise

In the scriptures at the beginning of this chapter, from the book of Chronicles, we see an example of how to gain victory in battle. Seek the face of God in prayer, listen for His instructions, and follow His directives. King Jehoshaphat and his people did something unusual in the war they faced. They strategically placed the praise leaders in front of the battle line, and they prevailed. Praise must be your initial weapon of choice in the battles of life. Praise is giving thanks to God during your trials and fiery situations. It is your willingness to honor God because He deserves your adoration, and it is also your approval of what God has done for you, in you, and through you.

You can express your praise to God in many ways. Praise is expressed through your words as you give thanks, when you shout His praises and sing to Him, in your applause, lifting of your hands in surrender, and through the instruments you play. When you raise your voice in songs to the Lord, songs from your heart and from your soul, you are giving God the praise He deserves.

Praise is also expressed through dance. When you abandon yourself to God in dance, you are indifferent about what others think and concerned only with what God thinks. Listen to these scriptures. *You turned my wailing into dancing. Psalm 30:11 (NIV). Let Israel rejoice in their Maker; let the people of Zion be glad in their King. Let them praise his name with dancing and make music to him with tambourine and harp. Psalm 149:23 (NIV). Praise Him with tambourine and dancing. Psalm 150:4a (NIV). A time to weep and a time to laugh, a time to mourn and a time to dance. Ecclesiastes 3:4 (NIV).*

Psalm 22:22 says, "You who fear the Lord, praise Him." God will destroy those who would oppose you because He inhabits the praises of His people. Praise will ensure your victory in the battle. It will help you to find joy no matter what you are feeling or facing. Praise him even when you do not feel like doing so; even when the answers are delayed and watch Him work powerfully in your situation. Praise gives God thanks and appreciation for His goodness and His tender mercies. Praise will still the enemy's attacks in your life but activate God in your battle. In the word praise is the word "raise." Praise will always raise you up in the battle no matter how devastating it might look or feel.

What things do I praise God for?

_____

_____

_____

_____

_____

_____

_____

_____

_____

Worship

If praise will make you victorious in battle, then worship will not only gain you victory, but it will catapult you into a deeper level of intimacy with God. As you begin to worship God, you step out of self to embrace the wonder and majesty of who God is and what He has done for you. This level of intimacy indicates you understand how to position yourself to win, because it gives you foresight into God's plan for your success. Someone defined intimacy as, "into me see." This simply means God sees and knows your heart and is concerned about the things that cause you pain, sorrow, and grief. He knows you are calling out to the only One who can deliver you out of the battle, and He will respond when you worship Him with all your heart and soul.

Worship is the adoration you give to God for who He is, His mighty acts, and tender mercies in your life. It is a demonstration of your complete devotion to Him when, in the darkest moments of your life, you take the time to steal away with Him to discover His plans for your deliverance. Worship is going to God with humility and standing in awe and wonder at His greatness; and it takes your focus off yourself in the battle and focuses your attention on the only One who can deliver you. It keeps you focused on your Source of help.

Worship reminds you help is on the way; and it is a time to lay aside your cares, worries, weights, and sins and go all the way with God. While the battle is raging and you begin to worship, you gain strength to lift your hands to God and you find power when you bow your knees in recognition of His goodness. While you are in the valley of the shadow of death, and you accept the fact what you are going through is only a shadow, it becomes evident a shadow cannot bring permanent hurt or damage to your life. When the battles are raging all around you and you feel you may not survive, you must remember God is still in control. He never lets go of you in the difficult and devastating moments of your life. It is during these difficult times He carries you close to His heart.

Worship – bow down in adoration and contemplation of who God is. In the word worship you find the word "ship." When you feel as if you are being tossed around in the battle like a ship on the sea, see yourself in a place of safety in God's presence where the waves, the winds, and the storms of life cannot touch you. Adore, reverence, respect, and honor Him during the battle. Trust God, instead of questioning Him. Praise and worship your way to victory during the battle!

_____

_____

_____

_____

_____

A Prayer of Praise and Worship

Father, thank You so much for providing a way for me to gain victory in the midst of the battle. Thank You for the weapons of praise and worship. Lord, as I worship You, I ask You to help me to overcome and be victorious in every battle I face. When I don't feel like praising and worshipping You, remind me as I press into You, I will find peace and rest in the midst of the battle. Show me how to move beyond what I feel into a place of worshipping You. Father, as I praise You, I ask You to lift the heavy burdens from my life and to bring me peace in the trials I face. Father, as I worship You, lead me into a deeper relationship with You. Let me know that in Your presence is safety from the storms raging in my life. You are my refuge, strength, and a present help in times of trouble. You have been my shield and buckler; my hiding place in the storms. Help me to run to You not murmuring and complaining but praising and worshipping You even when I cannot see my way clearly, because Your view is not cloudy.

I need Your help to press in closer when the enemy tries to pull me away with difficulties. You truly are my hiding place. You preserve me from trouble, and You surround me with songs of deliverance. I run to You so You can sing over me and comfort my soul during the storm. Thank You, Father, when I cannot call anyone else, You are always available and are only a breath away. Thank You for teaching me how to praise and worship You in the storms. In Jesus' name.

Amen!

A Life Enriched in Spite of the Battle
Chapter 21

Your life can be enriched no matter what battles come against you. This enrichment comes from God as you walk through the storms, and you are able to keep standing even while you are being tossed around. You are enriched in His presence; you are enriched with His plan; you are enriched by His grace; and you are enriched by His provision in all of life's circumstances. Let us look at Job's life, because his life was enriched even after enduring many battles.

In the land of Uz there lived a man whose name was Job. This man was blameless and up right; he feared God and shunned evil. He had seven sons and three daughters, and he owned seven thousand sheep, three thousand camels, five hundred yoke of oxen and five hundred donkeys, and had a large number of servants. He was the greatest man among all the people of the East. His sons used to take turns holding feasts in their homes, and they would invite their three sisters to eat and drink with them. When a period of feasting had run its course, Job would send and have them purified. Early in the morning he would sacrifice a burnt offering for each of them, thinking, "Perhaps my children have sinned and cursed God in their hearts." This was Job's regular custom.

Job 1:15 (NIV)

Battles are often fierce and destructive, and Job experienced both. Here was a godly, honorable, and upright man who loved and feared God, but he fought battles that raged out of control in his life. These battles were so fierce only God could help him. The story opens with Job doing all He could to cover the actions of his children and praying for their protection against wrong choices and evil practices. It is important to note Job was operating out of fear for his children. Because of this fear, he was driven to do all he could to protect them. One day Satan presented himself to the Lord along with the angels of God, and God questioned his presence. He told God he had come from roaming the earth. It seems he had been roaming around and was bored with what he found, so he was looking for someone or something to relieve his boredom. God said to Satan, "Have you considered my servant Job?" This sounds as if God was bragging on Job. He was telling Satan, here is a man who is filled with integrity, character, uprightness, and is also blameless before God. This was a man who stood in awe of God, who feared and revered Him. Satan countered God saying God had protected, blessed, and covered Job. He challenged God to stretch out His hand and strike everything Job had. He claimed Job would curse God to His face.

God gave Satan permission to test Job. The battles began to rage:

1. Job's oxen and livestock were stolen.

2. Fire fell from heaven and destroyed his servants.
3. His sheep were destroyed.
4. His camels were stolen.
5. His ten children were all killed.

All this took place not a day apart, not a week apart, nor even a year apart. The Bible says while each servant was giving his report, another servant came with a worse report than the first. The battles were raging out of control in Job's life. Finally, when Job heard his children were killed, he got up, tore his robe, shaved his head, and then fell on the ground and worshipped God. Job said, "*Naked I came from my mother's womb, and naked I will depart. The Lord gave and the Lord has taken away; may the name of the Lord be praised.*" (Job 1:21 NIV). You may be saying there goes that word "worship" again! Yes, Job worshipped while the battles were raging against him.

Satan lost the round on that day because Job did not complain in the midst of tragedy, grief and devastation; instead, he chose to worship God. I am sure Satan was very confused by his reaction. So, he went back to God and God said, "*Have you considered my servant Job?*" He told Satan, Job had still maintained his integrity even though Satan had tried to turn him against God. This time Satan challenged God that a man would give all he had to save his own life. God then gave Satan permission to bring affliction to Job with sickness, but he was not allowed to take Job's life. Satan left the presence of the Lord and brought sickness to Job's body. Job had sores from the top of his head to the soles of his feet. It was so bad he took a piece of pottery to scratch himself. By this time, Job's wife had had enough. She asked him if he was still holding on to his integrity and told him to, "*Curse God and die.*" It is clear his wife recognized the same thing in Job that God had pointed out to Satan. His integrity was evident for all to see. Job rebuked his wife for talking foolishly and questioned her about appreciating God only for the good and not in bad times.

What have been the effects of fear in my life?

_____
_____
_____
_____
_____
_____
_____
_____
_____
_____

I have read and studied the book of Job for many years and focused my attention so completely on Job it did not dawn on me, until I prepared this series of teachings, how much Job's wife also suffered. I simply brushed off her statement to Job as that of a foolish woman, not thinking she was also suffering. As I reflected on her part in this equation, I was reminded she was the one who had experienced the pain of giving birth to and then losing all ten children. Job lost all he had during these attacks, so she also lost her livelihood. She suffered right along with him, and in her pain spoke out how she felt about all the tragedies they had endured. God had not forgotten about her, He knew she was going to react the way she did, but He also knew Job would stand his ground and keep her steady despite the pain. I found one of the greatest scriptures in the entire Bible in the second chapter of Job. Chapter two verse ten says, "*In all of this, Job did not sin in what he said.*" Job was careful about his words during the battle. I know what happened to him was beyond his understanding, yet he kept a guard over his mouth and did not let the devil hear him complain against God.

What have been my complaints in the midst of hardship?

_____

_____

_____

_____

_____

_____

_____

_____

_____

_____

_____

Standing Strong in Difficulties

Job did not understand how he ended up in this situation, but he still did not give the devil the satisfaction of cursing God. Job's friends came to visit and to comfort him, but they were of no help. They simply could not believe someone who appeared to be so upright and blame less could be plunged into such a mess without having done anything wrong. They did not encourage him at all during his battle, but they added burdens upon him that he did not need during this time of testing. The storms raged mightily in Job's life, but he chose to worship God. He kept himself from murmuring and complaining. He suffered great agony yet held his peace. His friends questioned his relationship with God, but he remained steadfast. Job had a lot of questions for God, and he questioned God often. God took a long time before answering him; when God finally responded He did not answer or acknowledge any of Job's questions. Rather, many chapters later, we see God chose to question Job.

Then the Lord answered Job out of the storm. He said:

- *Who is this that darkens my counsel with words without knowledge?*
- *Brace yourself like a man; I will question you, and you shall answer me.*
- *Where were you when I laid the earth's foundation?*
- *Tell me if you understand. Who marked off its dimensions? Surely you know!*
- *Who stretched a measuring line across it?*
- *On what were its footings set, or who laid its cornerstone – while the morning stars sang together and all the angels shouted for joy?*
- *Who shut up the sea behind doors when it burst forth from the womb?*
- *When I made the clouds its garment and wrapped it in thick darkness, when I fixed limits for it and set its doors and bars in place, when I said, 'This far you may come and no farther; here is where your proud waves halt?"*

Job 38:111 (NIV)

God questioned Job from chapter thirty-eight all the way through chapter forty-one of the book of Job. God understood Job had gone through tremendous trials, difficulties, and complete devastation, but even though he had suffered, God was still God. God was Job's creator, and the created (Job) had no right to question God, the Creator, about His actions. Job learned God is God and He can allow and do what He pleases. Job repented and asked for forgiveness, he also forgave his friends who had unjustly accused him, and then God began to move in his situation.

What is my attitude in difficult seasons?

_____

_____

_____

_____

_____

_____

_____

_____

_____

Ending Strong

The latter years of Job's life were greater than his beginning. God gave him greater wealth than he had before, and He gave him ten more children. The Bible said his daughters were the most beautiful girls during that time. God added years to Job's life; he lived one hundred and forty years and saw four generations of his children's children. God blessed him immensely and gave him twice as much as he had before. When I reached the end of my study of Job, I stopped to ask the Lord a question. You may be asking some questions yourself after reading about the severity of the battles he encountered. My question to God was, "How was Job able to forget the loss of his previous ten children and move forward to enjoy the rest of his life?" I struggled with how he could have found peace after his storm, and I have wondered how he was able to continue serving God without being bitter and blaming Him for the destruction.

What kept Job faithful to his God? As I pondered on these questions, the Lord told me although the memories were still there, for Job to experience fullness and live out his life in peace, He had to remove the sting of the pain from his memory. The battle scars were still there, but the sting had been removed so Job was released from the painful memory. God knew he would not have survived and lived out his life in fullness, so He provided help and healing to Job. God took it a step further and He not only healed Job, but He made him whole and complete after the severity of his ordeal. He was freed from pain, fear, guilt, and shame; and he was able to receive the multiplied blessings from the Lord in his later years. God knows the battles you have endured. The enemy has also gone before God and asked about you, as well, and then tried to bring devastation to your life. Keep in mind the enemy cannot do anything to you without God knowing about it. He had to get permission prior to afflicting Job, even though Job opened the door because of fear for his children.

We also open doors, which allow the devil to attack and afflict us. Let me be very clear – God is not the one who attacks and devastates your life. The enemy is the one who brings the attacks. What the enemy means for evil God uses for your good, and during the attacks, He helps us develop compassion and humility. Trials, tribulations, and battles strengthen us and develop our faith. They keep us seeking God and waiting in His presence.

What questions do I need God to answer in my battle?

_____

_____

_____

_____

_____

_____

God Is Available

When you and I are on a mountaintop, we sometimes forget to pray, to praise, and to worship. We say, "Good morning God, see You later," and then we are gone. When all is going well in our world, we do not press into God and seek His face as consistently as we should. However, when a trial comes, and we know only God can deliver us, we seek Him diligently.

After you have gone through your battle, God will do for you what He did for Job. He will speak to you out of the storm (Job 38:1). This tells me He is in the storm with you; and He does not let you go into the battle alone. He is there when you arrive, ready to comfort and help you work your way to victory. God will also remove the sting of the pain from you so you can enjoy the rest of your life in peace and joy.

Job's life was enriched because, as he went through his battles and experienced God in a deeper way, he developed a deeper level of trust. Before the storms came, Job operated in fear concerning his children, but after going through the storm he learned to rely on God and to trust Him. In the battles Job developed an intimate relationship with God which gave him a testimony of the goodness of God. Your battles will bring you to a richer and deeper relationship with God. His grace during the battle will enrich your life, and His compassion will amaze you, when you discover He is with you during the storm. He is there to guide you and order your steps to the place where you are blessed beyond measure.

How has God demonstrated His availability to me in the storms?

_____

_____

_____

_____

_____

_____

_____

_____

How Do You Win?

Ephesians chapter six has provided the answer to this question with crystal clarity. You win by remembering you have been provided the tools to guarantee your success. Here is your winning strategy:

• Put on the full armor of God.
• Stand ready for battle, fully covered by the armor.
• Stand until you win.
• Close every door you have ever opened to the devil and send him packing.
• Know that you have God's protection.
• Remember you have been given authority to use the name of Jesus.
• Fight the good fight of faith. It is a good fight because you win. Jesus won it for you.
• Remember to put a guard over your mouth so you speak only the right words in your situation.
• Guard your heart and mind through Christ Jesus.
• When you have done all, rest in the faithfulness of God during the battle.
• Do not become weary in doing good because in due season you will reap if you don't faint.
• Finally, trust in the Lord with all your heart and lean not on your own understanding. In all your ways acknowledge Him and He will direct your path.

You Win!

How do I win in every battle that I face?

_____
_____
_____
_____
_____
_____
_____
_____
_____
_____

A Prayer for Enrichment

Father, in the name of Jesus, I thank You that You are always with me in every storm I face. As You were with Job, You are fully aware each time the enemy attacks me. Nothing takes You by surprise. Help me to know You are my protection in the battles of life. I ask You to help me put a guard over my mouth when the enemy sends his attacks to devastate my life. Help me to clearly see You will never abandon me, no matter what.

My hope is in Your steadfast love, mercy, and grace toward me. I am leaning on Your everlasting arms knowing they will always be there to support me, lift me, and cause me to soar even in the face of difficulties. I am grateful You are mindful of me, and You are concerned about everything that concerns me today. I pray when bad things happen in my life, I will know beyond a shadow of a doubt You are a good Father who does not bring bad things on His children.

Remind me bad things happen because of a world of sin. Enrich me in the battles of life. Help me to stand strong and firm when the battles are raging and remind me that my foundation is built on the solid rock of Jesus Christ. Thank You that I will always be enriched in Your presence, so I determine to come to You regularly because in You I find rest. In Jesus' name!

Amen!

A Daily Prayer for Protection

Father, in the name of Jesus, I thank You for providing for my protection in the battles of life. I thank You for teaching me about the armor of God that fully covers me in the battle. I am thankful for each day I can dress myself with Your protection. I make it my choice to put on the protection You have provided for me by simply speaking the Word of God over my situation. The Bible says when I speak Your Word, it will not return to me empty; but it will accomplish what I please and prosper where I send it. So, I boldly speak Your Word today as I put on the armor of God.

- Father, I put on the helmet of salvation, which keeps my mind covered from the attacks of the enemy.

- Father, I put on the breastplate of righteousness to guard my heart from the enemy's darts.

- Father, I put on the belt of truth, which is the Word of God, and I make the Word the center of my life.

- Father, I put on the shoes of peace to keep me steady in the midst of the battle. The shoes of peace will steady me in times of trouble.

- Father, I take the shield of faith so I can quench all the fiery darts of the wicked one.

- Father, I take up the sword of the spirit, which is Your Word, and I will use Your Word to nullify the work of the devil in my life, in Jesus' name.

- Father, I am praying always with all prayer and supplication to You because I know You are the One who answers my prayers.

I thank You that as I dress in the armor of Your protection, You will keep me from being annihilated in the battles of life. Thank You so much for Your precious gifts, in Jesus' name.

Amen!

A Prayer for Salvation

Father, I know without Jesus I am lost and without hope. I acknowledge You sent Jesus into the world to die for my sins. I believe He is Your Son, He was born of a virgin, and He died and then arose from the dead for my sins. I acknowledge I have sinned and fallen short of Your standards and ask You to forgive me.

I invite Jesus to come into my heart because the Bible says He is the only way, truth, and life, and no man comes to the Father but by Him. Father, I am coming to You in the precious name of Your Son, Jesus. I thank You now for saving me and setting me free, in Jesus' name.

Amen! (So Be It).

Notes

1. Chapters 15, 17, 18
   Rick Renner, Sparkling Gems from the Greek (Tulsa, OK: Teach all Nations, 2003)

2. Chapter 19
   Too Busy Not To Pray, Bill Hybels IVP Books, Downers Grove, Illinois

About The Author

Joan Murray is totally committed to helping people discover their destinies. She is the founder and CEO of Joan Murray Ministries and Seeds of Hope Worldwide Missions. Joan is dedicated to teaching, training, equipping and helping people who are in various life struggles.

Joan is an international Bible teacher, pastor, author, and missionary. She has travelled extensively throughout the United States and internationally sharing the gospel message and serving the needs of the downtrodden. Joan currently resides in Houston, Texas.

If you would like to know more about Joan Murray Ministries, please contact us at:

Joan Murray Ministries

P.O. Box 5073
Katy, TX 77491
281.398.2501

email: jmmcontactus@gmail.com
www.joanmurrayministries.org
www.jemmuniquegifts.com

Changing Lives Through the Power and Truth of God's Word.